CONTENTS

MAY 18, 2006

OPENING STATEMENT

WITNESSES

APPENDIX

Material Submitted for the Hearing Record

PHYSICIANS FOR UNDERSERVED AREAS ACT

HEARING

BEFORE THE

SUBCOMMITTEE ON IMMIGRATION, BORDER SECURITY, AND CLAIMS

OF THE

COMMITTEE ON THE JUDICIARY
HOUSE OF REPRESENTATIVES

ONE HUNDRED NINTH CONGRESS

SECOND SESSION

ON

H.R. 4997

MAY 18, 2006

Serial No. 109–111

Printed for the use of the Committee on the Judiciary

Available via the World Wide Web: http://judiciary.house.gov

U.S. GOVERNMENT PRINTING OFFICE

27–608 PDF WASHINGTON : 2006

For sale by the Superintendent of Documents, U.S. Government Printing Office
Internet: bookstore.gpo.gov Phone: toll free (866) 512–1800; DC area (202) 512–1800
Fax: (202) 512–2250 Mail: Stop SSOP, Washington, DC 20402–0001

COMMITTEE ON THE JUDICIARY

F. JAMES SENSENBRENNER, JR., Wisconsin, *Chairman*

HENRY J. HYDE, Illinois
HOWARD COBLE, North Carolina
LAMAR SMITH, Texas
ELTON GALLEGLY, California
BOB GOODLATTE, Virginia
STEVE CHABOT, Ohio
DANIEL E. LUNGREN, California
WILLIAM L. JENKINS, Tennessee
CHRIS CANNON, Utah
SPENCER BACHUS, Alabama
BOB INGLIS, South Carolina
JOHN N. HOSTETTLER, Indiana
MARK GREEN, Wisconsin
RIC KELLER, Florida
DARRELL ISSA, California
JEFF FLAKE, Arizona
MIKE PENCE, Indiana
J. RANDY FORBES, Virginia
STEVE KING, Iowa
TOM FEENEY, Florida
TRENT FRANKS, Arizona
LOUIE GOHMERT, Texas

JOHN CONYERS, JR., Michigan
HOWARD L. BERMAN, California
RICK BOUCHER, Virginia
JERROLD NADLER, New York
ROBERT C. SCOTT, Virginia
MELVIN L. WATT, North Carolina
ZOE LOFGREN, California
SHEILA JACKSON LEE, Texas
MAXINE WATERS, California
MARTIN T. MEEHAN, Massachusetts
WILLIAM D. DELAHUNT, Massachusetts
ROBERT WEXLER, Florida
ANTHONY D. WEINER, New York
ADAM B. SCHIFF, California
LINDA T. SÁNCHEZ, California
CHRIS VAN HOLLEN, Maryland
DEBBIE WASSERMAN SCHULTZ, Florida

PHILIP G. KIKO, *General Counsel-Chief of Staff*
PERRY H. APELBAUM, *Minority Chief Counsel*

SUBCOMMITTEE ON IMMIGRATION, BORDER SECURITY, AND CLAIMS

JOHN N. HOSTETTLER, Indiana, *Chairman*

STEVE KING, Iowa
LOUIE GOHMERT, Texas
LAMAR SMITH, Texas
ELTON GALLEGLY, California
BOB GOODLATTE, Virginia
DANIEL E. LUNGREN, California
JEFF FLAKE, Arizona
BOB INGLIS, South Carolina
DARRELL ISSA, California

SHEILA JACKSON LEE, Texas
HOWARD L. BERMAN, California
ZOE LOFGREN, California
LINDA T. SÁNCHEZ, California
MAXINE WATERS, California
MARTIN T. MEEHAN, Massachusetts

GEORGE FISHMAN, *Chief Counsel*
ART ARTHUR, *Counsel*
ALLISON BEACH, *Counsel*
CINDY BLACKSTON, *Professional Staff*
NOLAN RAPPAPORT, *Minority Counsel*

PHYSICIANS FOR UNDERSERVED AREAS ACT

THURSDAY, MAY 18, 2006

HOUSE OF REPRESENTATIVES,
SUBCOMMITTEE ON IMMIGRATION,
BORDER SECURITY, AND CLAIMS,
COMMITTEE ON THE JUDICIARY,
Washington, DC.

The Subcommittee met, pursuant to notice, at 2:04 p.m., in Room 2141, Rayburn House Office Building, the Honorable John N. Hostettler (Chairman of the Subcommittee) presiding.

Mr. HOSTETTLER. The Subcommittee will come to order.

Good afternoon. Today's hearing will examine H.R. 4997, the "Physicians for Underserved Areas Act." This legislation is sponsored by Congressman Jerry Moran, who has joined us today as a witness.

H.R. 4997 makes permanent the J-1 visa waiver program for physicians who agree to work in underserved areas—sometimes referred to as the "Conrad program" after the original author of the program, Senator Kent Conrad.

Under current law, foreign doctors may come to the United States to complete their residency training. Many do so using the J-1 visa, which is for cultural exchange and training programs.

One of the requirements for physicians who use the J visa is that the participant return to his or her country for 2 years upon completion of the training program in the United States. The purpose of this foreign residency requirement is to encourage American-trained physicians to return to their country and improve medical conditions there.

Since 1994, Congress has waived the 2-year foreign residency requirements for physicians who agree to work in an underserved area of the United States as designated by the Department of Health and Human Services. Each State receives 30 such waivers per year.

The waiver program allows States to recruit physicians to areas that may be considered unattractive to American physicians. Many communities that might otherwise have no access to medical services now have physicians nearby as a result of this program. It also responds to an overall shortage of physicians in the United States, a shortage that seems to be growing.

While today's hearing will address legislation to reauthorize a visa program for foreign physicians, I believe Congress must also focus on other ways to address the physician shortage. First, I am interested to hear from our witnesses today what is being done to increase the capacity of medical training programs here in the

United States. Educating more physicians here at home is one obvious way we can alleviate the shortage.

I'm also interested in the expansion of programs, such as the National Health Services Corps, which provides incentives for U.S. physicians to work in underserved areas.

In looking at the J-1 visa waiver program, we must keep in mind the intent behind the 2-year foreign residency requirement. We want to make sure that we aren't facilitating "brain drain" from countries that desperately need well-trained medical personnel.

In its 2006 World Health Report, the World Health Organization cited the migration of health care workers from poorer countries to richer countries as a major problem whose "consequences can be measured in lives lost."

J visas are designed to allow foreigners to participate in exchange and training programs here in the U.S. and then take those skills back to their home country. But right now, a significant portion of these physicians are staying here in the United States.

Another factor that is complicating the training goal of the J-1 visa program is that foreign physicians are now using the H-1B visa to come to the U.S. for their residencies. Physicians who come to the U.S. on an H-1B visa for the residency training are not required to return to their home country for 2 years.

As a result, foreign physicians prefer to use the H-1B and fewer are using the J-1 visa. With fewer physicians using the J-1 program, there are fewer available physicians to participate in the J-1 waiver program to work in underserved areas, and there are also fewer physicians returning to needier countries.

I believe we need to closely examine this disparity in treatment and consider a uniform policy for foreign physicians who receive training in the U.S. The J-1 visa waiver program may be helpful in getting physicians to underserved areas, but it is, hopefully, a temporary fix to a much larger problem.

I am hopeful that this Committee and other Committees of jurisdiction will work to find ways to educate and train greater numbers of American physicians and reduce our reliance on foreign physicians.

At this time, the Chair recognizes the gentlelady from Texas, the Ranking Member of the Subcommittee, Ms. Jackson Lee, for purposes of an opening statement.

Ms. JACKSON LEE. Thank you very much, Mr. Chairman.

I appreciate this hearing. I appreciate the witnesses. And you have certainly crafted or laid the parameters down that it is complex, but it's a good program.

And the legislation that my friend and colleague Mr. Moran has, has great merit because we do know that there are certain concerns that you've expressed that I join you in. We don't want to have a brain drain of some of our developing nations all over the world. In fact, we want to be partners in good health care.

But at the same time, we want to ensure the normal flow of talented physicians in underserved areas, and I might say, with a State as big as Texas, we're already asking for an increase or a need that would cover the vast State—vast areas of our State.

So we know that we have to find a way to answer your concerns to discern the purpose of the utilization of other visas versus the

J-1. We have to address the question of overstays, and I might say we have to address the question of training more American doctors, helping our Nation's medical schools, and providing resources for nurses in America, and training and teachers.

But I do believe that this is a valuable program, and I'm delighted that the GAO is present, Mr. Chairman, because I do want to acknowledge, as you well know, that Senator Conrad and myself asked for a GAO study to assess where we are in this program and how we can make it effective. And I look forward to your testimony.

I mentioned, again, the legislation of Congressman Jerry Moran that was introduced just recently, H.R. 4997. And specifically, it would make the J-1 visa program permanent.

The J visa is used for one of the educational cultural exchange programs that has become a gateway for foreign medical graduates to gain admission to the United States as non-immigrants for the purpose of graduate medical education training. The visa that most of these physicians enter under is the J-1 non-immigrant visa.

And let me just say this. I had the opportunity to speak before the National Convention of Indo-American Physicians and Pakistan Physicians. They are what the oath that they take represents. They're healers. They want to do what is right.

But I tell you, one of the number-one issues was what was happening to the J-1 visa because they wanted to use it in a positive sense. And I made a commitment in a legislative manner, which is to say that this Congress would take the J-1 visa program seriously and know of their interest and passion.

One of the doctors in particular was Dr. Kudir, who has formerly served—or has served as the leadership of the Pakistan-American doctors. But they wanted it to be constructive. And they are participants in making the J-1 visa work, not to abuse it. And I think we should engage physicians and those who participate in this program to make it work.

The physicians who participate in the J-1 visa programs are required to return to their home country for a period of at least 2 years before they can apply for another non-immigrant visa or legal permanent resident status, unless they're granted a waiver of this requirement.

In 1994, Senator Kent Conrad established a new basis for waiver of this requirement with an amendment to the Immigration and Nationality Act. It was known as then as the Conrad State 20 program. It permitted each State to obtain waivers for 20 physicians by establishing that they were needed in health professional shortage areas known as HPSAs.

On November 2, 2002, the Conrad 20 program was extended to 2004, and the number of waivers available to the States were increased to 30. This program, which is now referred to as the "Conrad 30" or "State 30" program, expired on June 1, 2004.

On December 3, 2004, it was reinstated and extended to June 1, 2006. That is why we're here today, which is only a few weeks from now. Congressman Moran's Physicians for Underserved Areas Act would eliminate the need for future extensions by making the program permanent.

And I might say because of the recounting of the yearly or every other year extension, it might make sense that we have the parameters and the strictures or the structure of the program such that we can address the permanent aspect of it.

When the Conrad 30 Program was established in 1994, most of those studying the supply of physicians in the United States were concerned about the distribution of physicians, as opposed to the total number of doctors being trained. It is now generally recognized that we're facing a severe physician shortage. The Health Policy Institute eliminates—estimates that the shortage could grow to as much as 200,000 by 2020, an astounding possibility in view of the fact that the physician population in the United States currently is only about 800,000.

And might I say that I am not bragging about this catastrophe, it is one. Obviously, we have to do something outside the jurisdiction of this Committee with our Nation's medical schools, the encouragement of physicians or medical students, and certainly health care in America.

But given where we are today, this is a needed program. The failure to forecast this severe physician shortage may explain why from 1980 until last year no new medical schools opened in the United States. According to the Health Policy Institute, the United States needs to produce an extra 10,000 physicians per year over the next decade and a half in order to meet the demands of the country.

This number assumes that the number of foreign-educated physicians will remain constant. We might need to have "hug a physician" day in America.

Senator Conrad and I have asked the General Accountability Office to do a survey of State views on the Conrad 30 program. All 50 States filled out a GAO questionnaire and promptly returned it to the GAO. One of the GAO investigators will testify about the results of that survey, and so I'll look forward to that.

Approximately 80 percent of the States reported that the annual limit of 30 waivers per State is inadequate. Only 13 percent reported that it is inadequate. Excuse me. I'm sorry. Eighty percent of the States reported that the annual limit of 30 waivers per State is adequate, and only 13 percent said it was inadequate.

Eleven States estimated that they need between 5 and 50 more waiver physicians, which would total 200 more waiver physicians. Forty-four States did not use all of their allotted, and the total of the unused waivers for the year was 664, which is one of my views of being able to move some of the waivers from State to State.

The J-1 visa program has been in effect now for more than a decade. In addition to being a good source of additional physicians, it ensures that additional physicians will go where they are most needed, health professional shortage areas in both rural and urban settings.

I can assure you, Mr. Chairman and to this Committee, that it is important for us to have this hearing, but more importantly, to take it seriously and to address the concerns of our States, but also Americans who need good health care.

And I look forward to admitting certain letters, but I will hold them for the witnesses' testimony, and I believe that, together, we can make this program effective and provide the good health care for all Americans.

With that, I yield back.

Mr. HOSTETTLER. I thank the gentlelady.

The Chair will now introduce members of our panel of witnesses.

The Honorable Jerry Moran began his career in public service in the Kansas State Senate, serving 8 years in that body, including 2 years as majority leader. As the representative in Congress of Kansas's 1st District, which has more hospitals than any congressional district in the country, Mr. Moran has been a leading advocate for health care reform, rural health care in particular.

Congressman Moran has been supportive of community health care centers and has introduced additional measures, such as the Community Pharmacy Preservation Act, which seeks to keep small-town pharmacies open and accessible.

His efforts in Congress have earned Mr. Moran the top legislative award from the National Rural Health Association. He is the sponsor of the bill H.R. 4997, the legislation that this panel is discussing today.

Edward S. Salsberg began his career in public health in 1984 at the New York State Department of Public Health, where he served as a bureau director. In 1996, Mr. Salsberg left the department to found the Center for Health Workforce Studies at the School of Public Health of the University at Albany of the State University of New York, where he served as its executive director.

Mr. Salsberg has authored and co-authored numerous reports on the health care workforce and has spoken throughout the country on the topic. He currently serves as director of the Center for Workforce Studies at the Association of American Medical Colleges.

John B. Crosby became the executive director of the American Osteopathic Association in May 1997. Prior to joining the AOA, he spent 6 years at the American Medical Association as senior vice president for health policy, where he was actively involved with policy development and strategic planning.

He currently serves on the board of directors of the Chicago Health Policy Research Council and the Health Care Quality Alliance in Washington, D.C. Mr. Crosby has worked on health care issues for both the private and public sectors since 1977. He has served in positions at think tanks, trade associations, and on Capitol Hill.

Leslie G. Aronovitz began her service to the U.S. Government Accountability Office at GAO's Atlanta office in 1974. Before working on health and income security issues, Ms. Aronovitz was an assistant director in GAO's Accounting and Financial Management Division. There, she directed much of GAO's work on the quality of audits performed by public accountants. This work led to important changes in the way the accounting profession engaged in self-monitoring.

Ms. Aronovitz has served as director of GAO's health care team for the past 15 years. Among her numerous responsibilities as director of the team is research on health professions shortages.

Gentlemen and lady, we appreciate your presence here today, and you will notice we have the light system, and we ask—and without objection, your entire written testimony will be made a part of the record.

If you can keep within that 5 minutes as much as possible, we will give an opportunity for the panel to ask questions.

Congressman Moran, you are recognized.

TESTIMONY OF THE HONORABLE JERRY MORAN, A REPRESENTATIVE IN CONGRESS FROM THE STATE OF KANSAS

Mr. MORAN. Mr. Chairman, thank you very much. Thank you for the privilege of appearing before your Subcommittee today.

I appreciate your comments and am pleased to support your effort to broaden the inquiry about increasing the availability of health care professionals across the country. I appreciate Ms. Jackson Lee and her efforts; we were engaged as allies the last time this program was reauthorized in 2002.

I've been a Member of Congress now for a decade. Much of my focus in Washington has been about access to health care. I represent one of the most rural districts in the country. My largest community is a population about 45,000.

I represent three quarters of the geography of Kansas, and you are correct. We have 75 hospitals in the congressional district, more than any congressional district in the Nation.

My constituents drive long distances to access health care. They are elderly, generally, and income levels are—would be below the national average. I have been engaged in the Rural Health Care Coalition and its efforts since coming to Congress and have served as its chairman for a number of years.

My colleague in co-sponsoring this bill, Mr. Pomeroy, the gentleman from North Dakota, is the co-chairman of the Rural Health Care Coalition today.

This issue is one that I think matters so much. In fact, I believe that health care is the number-one domestic issue we face in the country today. And it is about access, but it's also about affordability.

And I have been involved in the J-1 visa program since coming to Congress. Many of the physicians who serve, who provide health care services to my constituents, are J-1 visa doctors.

And you were right in your recitation of the history. This has—came about, this program came about in 1994. We've also had a companion Federal J-1 visa program. And surprising to me and perhaps to others, Kansas was not a participant in the J-1 visa program on the State level until 2002. Prior to that, we relied upon the United States Department of Agriculture to provide J-1 visa access through the Federal program.

And since 2002, when we started the Conrad—now Conrad 30 program, we have provided 66 physicians to the people of our State. The population of America is 25 percent rural, and yet physicians, their practice, only 10 percent of practicing physicians have their practice in rural America. So there's a tremendous shortage.

Having outlined the rural nature of my district and my focus in Congress, I also would like to point out that the J-1 visa program is important to urban areas of the country. It is not just a rural issue. Many of the core centers of our cities face the same dilemma in trying to attract and retain physicians.

It's been my experience that if you are a physician who is primarily interested in making money, you will not locate in the core of a center of a city. You will not locate in rural America because the population base, the patient load is generally older. That means that Medicare has a significant component of your practice.

In fact, of the 75 hospitals, many of the hospitals in our congressional district—certainly 60, 70, 80, sometimes even 90 percent of the patients that are admitted to our hospitals are on Medicare, which means that Medicare is the sole—is nearly the sole provider of the revenue necessary to generate income for the hospital or the physician.

And then on top of that, you add Medicaid, which also is a detriment to a physician's income. Underserved areas exist in this country, and they exist for a number of reasons, cultural as well as economic.

This has been a successful program in Kansas since its arrival in 2002. I know of a number of communities, and I've talked to constituents who tell me that but "absent that J-1 physician being in my community, I would not be alive today."

So it's a matter of economic growth and community development, but it is a matter of life and death that people can access a physician, and in many cases, it's a J-1 visa physician within the confines of their community.

Rush County Memorial Hospital is located about 25 miles from my hometown. Thirty-seven hundred people live in the county. They have three J-1 visa physicians. One now, two—a husband and wife team, who have now retired. That community has been served by J-1 visa physicians for a number of years—decades, in fact—since the J-1 visa program was—arrived, and they now have a physician who has replaced the two who retired.

Greensburg, Kansas, population 1,500. For the last 10 years, the only physicians they've had in the county are J-1 visa physicians. In each of these cases, the community has attempted, at least initially, to attract a United States, an American physician without success.

Meade County District Hospital, population of the county is about 1,600, 1,700, they made that attempt. Finally were successful in obtaining a J-1 visa physician through the waiver program. That doctor is now from Romania, has stayed at the hospital for 6 years. When he retired and left the community, they attracted a J-1 visa physician from the Maldives Islands.

And finally, the hope—I'm, as you indicated, a supporter of community health care clinics. I think they're part of access to health care. They're also a part of a way that we can reduce health care costs.

And United Methodist Ministries in Garden City, Kansas, which serves a very diverse population, has now been able to attract a J-1 visa doctor, originally from Peru, who is bilingual and is arriving in August of this year to provide services to those with—really, without any insurance, without any financial means. And it's only through this J-1 visa program that this community health clinic has been successful in attracting a physician.

Mr. Chairman, I am an advocate, a supporter, a—just an enthusiastic, and I guess it's not just—it's not based upon emotion. It's based upon the reality that absent this program, people will not be living, communities will not survive, and rural America as well as urban America will have one more nail in its coffin.

So I urge the reauthorization of this program. I'm happy to discuss potential amendments in a way that we can meet the needs perhaps of Texas, which has perhaps a greater demand than the 30 that are allowed, the flexibility to move physicians around the country, but also the permanent nature.

Again, this is an issue that I've lived from the beginning of my time in Congress, and it would be nice to have a permanent program as compared to us rushing in here always at the last minute, trying to get the J-1 visa program reauthorized for a short period of time.

I thank the Chairman and the Ranking Member and the gentleman from California for their attention.

[The prepared statement of Mr. Moran follows:]

PREPARED STATEMENT OF THE HONORABLE JERRY MORAN, A REPRESENTATIVE IN CONGRESS FROM THE STATE OF KANSAS

I am here today to discuss H.R. 4997, the Physicians for Underserved Areas Act, which would reauthorize the J-1 Visa Waiver program. The J-1 Visa Waiver program provides opportunities for graduates of foreign medical schools, who have trained in U.S. medical residency programs on the J-1 cultural exchange visa, to stay in the United States if they serve for three years in an area that has a health professional shortage. These designated health professional shortage areas can occur in rural areas as well as urban areas.

State government agencies may sponsor J-1 physician waiver requests under the State 30 program. The State 30 program is designed to provide each State up to 30 waivers for physicians each year. Each State has been given some flexibility to implement its own guidelines, but there are some basic requirements that are common to all State 30 programs. The recruitment process takes into consideration the 'fit' with the practice, the community, and the needs of the physician and family.

One of my goals is improving access to health care in rural areas. It is extremely difficult to recruit health care professionals to places where doctors are few and access to major metropolitan hospitals requires hours of travel. According to the U.S. Department of Health and Human Services, while a quarter of the population lives in rural areas, only 10 percent of physicians practice there. This definitely highlights the need for the J-1 Visa Waiver program. Today, I would like to highlight how this program has benefited my home state of Kansas and the predominately rural area which I represent.

Kansas has been able to recruit 66 physicians to work in underserved areas and with underserved populations since 2002. Each year, the interest has grown and more and more physicians and hospitals are finding that this match is benefiting not only themselves, but the communities which they serve.

The Rush County Memorial Hospital located in La Crosse, Kansas is responsible for providing health care to the 3,700 residents of the county. With a population that is primarily elderly, having quality healthcare is a major concern and requirement.

After advertising and spending countless dollars and resources trying to recruit American born, American trained doctors, Rush County Memorial turned to the J-1 Visa program to meet their healthcare needs. They have been able to recruit three J-1 Visa physicians into the area and would not be able to have top notch healthcare without this program. In addition, the physicians have been welcomed into the community and warmly received. One physician has stated that this small Midwestern town reminds him of his home community in Egypt and has started to put down roots by buying a home and getting involved in community events. The J-1 Visa Waiver program has been invaluable to the Rush County Memorial Hospital.

Greensburg, Kansas is a small, rural community which has had difficulty recruiting physicians in the past. For the last 10 years, their physicians have all been J-1 physicians. They have served the community well and have been providing excellent health care. The current J-1 physician manages 3 mid-level practitioners, provides health care to the local assisted living facility and provides care at the mental health facility which is located 10 miles from his place of residence. However, he still finds time to work a booth at the local health fair. For this community, it is imperative that the J-1 Visa Waiver program be permanently reauthorized.

For 15 years, the Meade District Hospital has tried to get an American born, American trained physician to move to their rural Southwest Kansas hospital and have had no luck. However, through their participation in the J-1 Visa Waiver program, they have been able to attract foreign born physicians for the last 10 years. The J-1 Visa program has helped the hospital provide quality care to their patients. They had one doctor, originally from Romania, who stayed in the hospital for six years and a current doctor from the Maldaise Islands who they anticipate having a long term relationship with as well. The J-1 Visa program has been a lifesaver to this hospital and the citizens of Meade County.

Finally, the last success story I will highlight is the story of the United Methodist Mexican-American Ministries which is located in Garden City, Kansas. They are scheduled to receive their first J-1 Visa doctor in August of this upcoming year. This community health clinic provides care for many migrant and immigrant families who speak a variety of languages including Spanish, German, and French. The new J-1 Visa doctor is originally from Peru and is highly educated, bi-lingual and has tremendous references. The private medical community has been supportive of the clinic's efforts to recruit a doctor as the need for medical care is great in this area of Kansas. Without the J-1 Visa program, this clinic would not be able to get a physician to treat their patients.

People deserve quality health care regardless of their location. The J-1 Visa Waiver program is helping many hospitals in my district find qualified physicians for their communities and this increases the quality of healthcare overall in Kansas. This is a well regarded, well run program that is worthy of permanent reauthorization. The Physicians for Underserved Areas Act is the way to make this happen.

Mr. HOSTETTLER. Thank you, Congressman Moran.

Even though that I must admit that it is a blessing from time to time to see your beaming face in front of this Committee, that being said——

Mr. MORAN. Mr. Chairman, I might remind you that I was on the steering Committee that allowed you to come to the Judiciary Committee. [Laughter.]

And I appreciate that very much because you were senior to me in the House Agriculture Committee, and you allowed me to become a Subcommittee Chairman when you departed. And I'm very grateful for your—for your move.

Mr. HOSTETTLER. And now we know "the rest of the story."

Mr. Salsberg?

TESTIMONY OF EDWARD SALSBERG, DIRECTOR, CENTER FOR WORKFORCE STUDIES, ASSOCIATION OF AMERICAN MEDICAL COLLEGES

Mr. SALSBERG. Good afternoon, Chairman Hostettler and Ranking Member Jackson Lee and other Members of the Subcommittee.

My name is Ed Salsberg. I'm the director of the Center for Workforce Studies at the Association of American Medical Colleges.

AAMC represents all 125 accredited U.S. allopathic medical schools, nearly 400 teaching hospitals and health systems, and 94 academic societies.

I've been asked to address today the likely future supply and demand for physician services and what our medical schools and teaching hospitals are doing to assure an adequate supply of physicians to meet America's needs.

Let me state at the outset that the AAMC and our members are fully committed to assuring an adequate supply of well-trained physicians to serve the Nation. Historically, U.S. medical schools have responded to the needs of the public and policymakers, especially when those needs have been clearly articulated and supported by Government programs and policies.

In the 1960's and 1970's, the U.S. medical school enrollment doubled in response to a national need and Federal support. In the 1980's and 1990's, allopathic medical schools responded to a series of Government reports that clearly expressed concern about a pending surplus. And the schools are now responding to growing evidence about a future shortage, including the recent report by the National Council on Graduate Medical Education.

While we believe our members will respond, we believe more can be done, including in terms of Federal support for our efforts. Forecasting future physician supply and demand is extremely difficult. We're trying to look 10, 20 years out into the future, and there are just many, many unknowns.

But based on our current analysis, we believe that the Nation is likely to face a significant shortage in the future. That's really reflecting both factors of supply and demand.

On the supply side, we know there are 250,000 active physicians over the age of 55 that will be approaching age of retirement. We know that there are reports of younger physicians not interested in working the long hours that physicians did in the past.

On the demand side, the Nation is growing rapidly, adding 25 million additional Americans every decade. We know that the elderly will double between 2000 and 2030. That's critical because the elderly use far more services than a younger population.

And I think also the increasing wealth of the Nation and the expectations of the baby boom generation lead us to conclude the demand for health services, particularly physician services, will be rising in the future and that the supply will not be keeping up.

A comment about international medical school graduates who are really a critical source of—component of the physician workforce. International medical school graduates represent 25 percent of our active physicians in America and 25 percent of the physicians in training.

As you mentioned, we are hearing of growing concerns internationally about the impact of the migration of physicians from less developed to more developed countries, and this is an issue of concern.

The AAMC has recommended a number of actions to better assure an adequate supply of physicians in the coming years. First, last February, the association adopted a position of recommending that U.S. medical schools increase their enrollment by 15 percent.

We're now considering a recommendation to our members that they increase enrollment by 30 percent. That would be equal to about 5,000 additional graduates each year. We've seen some response already, and I'll come back to that.

A second important step would be to raise the caps on Medicare-funded GME positions. Our medical schools are beginning to respond, but they're clearly concerned that in the absence of an increase in the cap on residency positions, that their efforts to increase the physician supply will not lead to that end.

Third, we reiterated our commitment to the importance of having a diverse, culturally diverse physician workforce that reflects the Nation.

Fourth, we've recommended and feel it's critical that we expand the National Health Service Corps. That really is probably the most effective national strategy to assure redistribution of physicians to underserved areas.

And fifth, we support efforts to expand data collection and analysis on an ongoing basis to assure that the medical community and the public are aware of what the future physician workforce needs are.

In that regard, we are concerned with the elimination last year of about 50 percent of title 7 funding, one of the only sources of funding for medical education, including medical education in rural communities. And also eliminated was the support for the national center and the regional centers for health workforce data collection.

Let me just note that the U.S. medical schools are responding. More than half of the U.S. allopathic schools have indicated their plans or serious consideration for expanding over the next several years. We also expect to see five new allopathic schools in the coming years.

Overall, we see about a 10 percent increase in U.S. medical school enrollment in the pipeline now, and we hope to see more.

I think—in closing, I think U.S. medical schools have begun to respond to the calls for an expansion. We could use your support. A positive signal from the Federal Government, such as the restoration of title 7 funding, lifting of the Medicare GME caps, and expansion of the National Health Service Corps would go a long way to inform and support the efforts of U.S. medical schools to expand their capacity.

I thank you for the opportunity to speak to you today and would welcome any questions.

[The prepared statement of Mr. Salsberg follows:]

Prepared Statement of Edward Salsberg

AAMC

Statement

Association of American Medical Colleges
2450 N Street, N.W., Washington, D.C. 20037-1127
T 202 828 0400 F 202 828 1125
www.aamc.org

Jordan J. Cohen, M.D.
President

Legislative Hearing on

H.R. 4997: "Physicians for Underserved Areas Act"

Testimony to

United States House of Representatives
Committee on the Judiciary
Subcommittee on Immigration, Border Security, and Claims

by

Edward Salsberg
Director, Center for Workforce Studies
Association of American Medical Colleges
May 18, 2006

Good afternoon, Chairman Hostettler and members of the Subcommittee.

My name is Edward Salsberg, I am the Director of the Center for Workforce Studies at the Association of American Medical Colleges (AAMC). Thank you for this opportunity to speak to you today regarding the physician workforce and the response of America's allopathic medical schools and teaching hospitals to a growing concern about potential future physician shortages.

The AAMC is a nonprofit association representing all 125 accredited U.S. allopathic medical schools; nearly 400 major teaching hospitals and health systems, including Department of Veterans Affairs medical centers; and 94 academic and scientific societies. Through these institutions and organizations, the AAMC represents 109,000 faculty members, 67,000 medical students, and 104,000 resident physicians.

Our mission is to improve the health of the public by enhancing the effectiveness of academic medicine. Together with our members we pursue this mission through the education of the physician and medical scientist workforce, the discovery of new medical knowledge, the development of innovative technologies for prevention, diagnosis and treatment of disease, and the delivery of health care services in academic settings. The AAMC is committed to promoting an adequate supply of well-educated physicians sufficient in number and competencies to meet likely future needs of Americans.

The AAMC established its Center for Workforce Studies in 2004 to enhance and make publicly available more sophisticated data and analysis regarding the supply of and demand for physicians. The Center is committed to providing the medical education community (medical schools, medical students, residency programs and teaching hospitals), the public and policy makers with better information on current and likely future physician workforce needs. The Center does this through original research, analysis of existing data, collaboration with other associations representing physicians and through an annual conference on physician workforce research. The information on future workforce needs is intended to help guide decision making in the medical education community and where necessary, inform and promote public policies to help assure an appropriate supply of well prepared physicians. The Center has already produced a number of reports including:

- Medical School Expansion Plans: Results of the AAMC 2005 Survey of U.S. Medical Schools;
- Recent Reports and Studies of Physician Shortages in the U.S.;
- Key Physician Data by State.

These reports and additional information on the Center are available at: http://www.aamc.org/workforce .

In my comments today, I want to provide you with some basic background on the physician workforce, why we are concerned about the likelihood of a future physician shortage, what the AAMC is recommending in terms of physician workforce policies, and finally, how the nation's allopathic medical schools and teaching hospitals are responding.

Background on the Supply of Physicians

The vast majority of licensed physicians in the U.S. are educated in allopathic schools—those that confer an MD degree—and residency training programs in the nation's teaching hospitals accredited by the Accreditation Council for Graduate Medical Education (ACGME). Allopathic medical schools and their affiliated teaching hospitals are a critical source of research, new medical knowledge, and clinical care, and are a vital part of the nation's medical safety net.

Physicians in the United States can practice medicine only after completion of a medical degree ("undergraduate medical education"), and at least one year of post-graduate training in an accredited residency program ("graduate medical education" or GME). About 16,000 physicians graduate from U.S. allopathic medical schools every year with an MD degree; they fill about two-thirds of first-year residency positions in training programs—such as internal medicine, general surgery, pediatrics, and others—that are accredited by the ACGME. Graduates of foreign medical schools, generally referred to as international medical school graduates or IMGs, represent about 25% of the new residents each year; and about 1 in 4 of these IMGs are U.S. citizens who attended schools outside of the U.S. Graduates of osteopathic medical schools (DOs) represent about 11% of all physicians entering graduate training each year. About two-thirds of DOs enter ACGME accredited residency programs. Physicians in the U.S. are licensed by individual states, all of whom require an MD or DO degree, as well as some level of accredited graduate training (GME). The figure below presents the distribution of the physicians entering training in the U.S. in 2004.

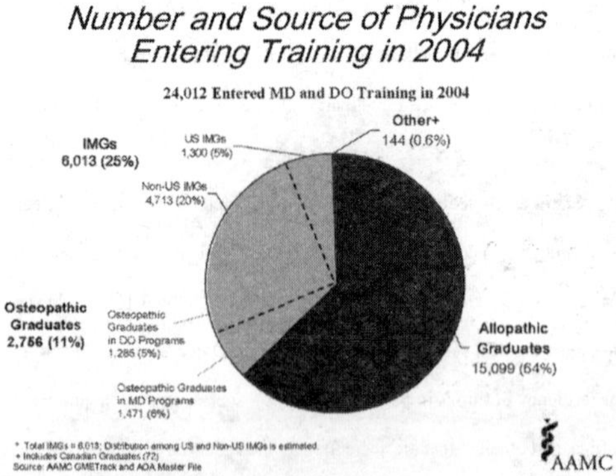

In 2005, there were almost 850,000 physicians active in medicine in the U.S., including about 101,000 in residency training and nearly 60,000 osteopaths. About 24% of active physicians in the US are graduates of non-U.S. medical schools.

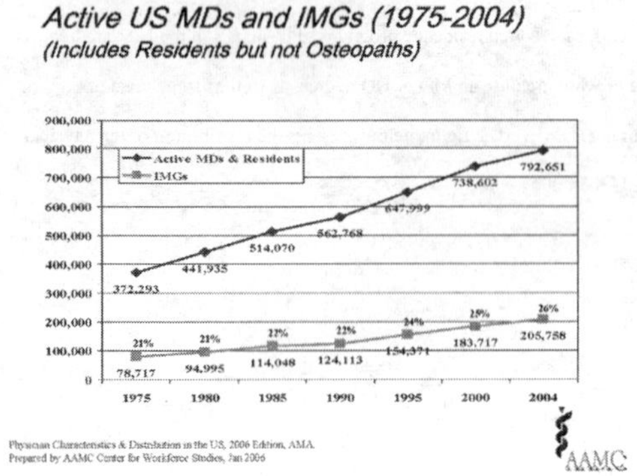

Why a Physician Shortage Is Likely

The expected future shortage of physicians is driven by likely changes in both the supply and the demand for physicians. On the demand side, key factors include: (1) the growing U.S. population; (2) the rapid growth in people over the age of 65 (those that consume the greatest resources); and (3) the rising expectations of Americans along with increasing wealth that will motivate and enable them to use more services. On the supply side, key factors include: (1) the aging of the physician workforce (1 of 3 active physicians over the age 55 and they are likely to retire by 2020); and (2) a new generation of physicians who may not be willing to work the long hours that prior generations of physicians have worked. At current levels of training, the physician–to-population ratio will peak by 2020 and then fall, just as the baby boomers begin to reach 75 years of age.

A dozen states already report physician shortages or expect shortages within the next decade; nationally, at least a dozen specialties report similar shortages.[1] These shortages are likely to exacerbate the existing lack of access for the 20 percent of Americans that live in government designated Health Professional Shortage Areas (HPSA).[2] Many rural and urban communities, economically disadvantaged, and underrepresented minority populations are likely to remain medically under-served for the foreseeable future, and certainly will be more under served if a national shortage emerges.

---

[1] http://www.aamc.org/meded/cfws/icutwrkfce.pdf
[2] http://bhpr.hrsa.gov/shortage/

The Supply of Physicians

For the last 50 years, the physician–to-population ratio has been growing steadily. This reflects a doubling in medical school enrollment in the 1960s and 1970s. The nation's physician supply is still rising due to the higher levels of enrollment established in that period. But with the report of the Graduate Medical Education National Advisory Commission (GMENAC) in the late 1970s predicting a large surplus of physicians, allopathic enrollment stabilized. In fact, the number of graduates from U.S. allopathic schools has been virtually flat since 1980. As a result, a very large number of active physicians are now nearing retirement age. If historical retirement patterns continue, the annual number of physicians retiring each year will grow from less than 9,000 in 2000 to over 22,000 a year by 2020, slightly less than the number of new physicians completing training annually in 2005.

The near-zero growth in U.S. MD graduates has translated to a sharp decrease in the number of allopathic educational slots per population in America. In fact, between 1980 and 2005, the US population grew by more than 70 million (31%)[3] while there was no growth in allopathic enrollment; this has led to a significant and steady decline in enrollment per 100,000 population.

[3] US Census. http://www.census.gov/ipc/www/usinterimproj/natprojtab02a.pdf Accessed May 15, 2006

Allopathic Graduation Trends

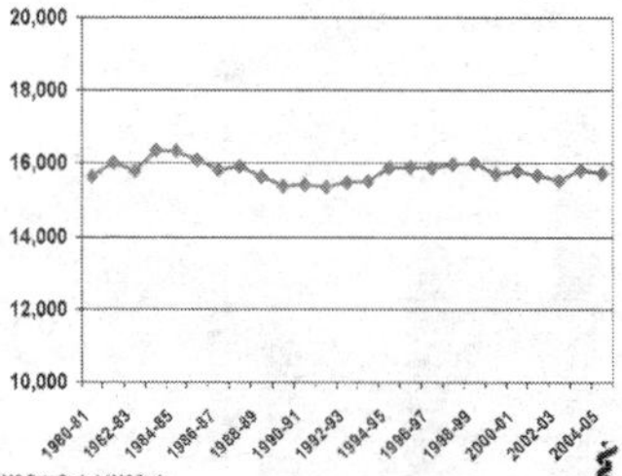

Source: AAMC Data Book, AAMC Facts
Prepared by AAMC, Center for Workforce Studies, Jan 2006

AAMC

Per Capita MD Enrollment Has Fallen Since 1980

First Year Enrollment per 100,000

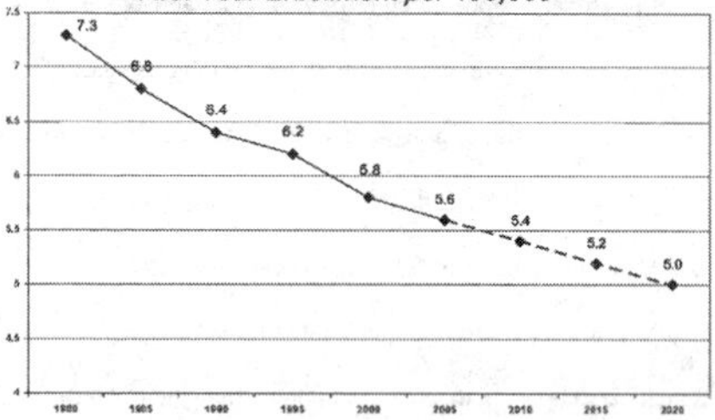

Source: AAMC Data Book; US Census Bureau.
Prepared by Center for Workforce Studies, AAMC, Feb 2006.

AAMC

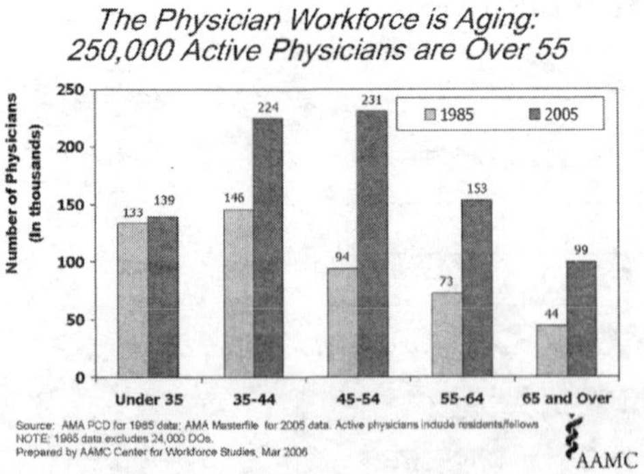

In addition to the large number of physicians approaching retirement age, there are growing reports that the newest generation of physicians do not want to work the long hours of physicians in the past. Gender plays a role. While only 10% of practicing physicians were female in 1980, they are now about 50% of the medical students. While this trend is encouraging from a societal perspective, it has implications for the physician workforce because women tend to work fewer hours than their male counterparts. Moreover, there are growing reports that many of today's young physicians, male and female, are choosing to work fewer hours than their older counterparts regardless of their gender. As a result, the future physician workforce may effectively be 10% lower than their aggregate numbers may suggest.

Because of the enormous potential impact on supply of both changes in retirement patterns by older physicians and work hours by younger physicians, the AAMC Center for Workforce

Studies in collaboration with the AMA and numerous physician specialty associations, is currently conducting surveys of older and younger physicians to obtain more detailed data on their practice patterns.

International Medical School Graduates (IMGs)

IMGs have been a critical component of the physician workforce serving Americans for many decades. For the past 30 years, between 4,000 and 6,500 IMGs have entered the American health care system every year by entering an ACGME accredited residency (GME) program. Currently the number is near 6,500. While IMGs come to the U.S. on many types of visas, the vast majority stay in the U.S. after completing their training. In recent years, the number of U.S. citizen-IMGs has been increasing, with the majority going to for-profit medical schools in the Caribbean. In 2006, about 1,400 US IMGs will enter residency training in the U.S. Little information is available about the number that actually leave the U.S. to attend school, but we do know that about 2,500 are applying each year to take the exam required of all IMGs who want to enter GME in the U.S.

One of the most common visas among IMGs in training is the J-1 visa. The formal name of the J-1 visa program is the "Exchange Visitor Sponsorship Program". It was established to train physicians from other countries to share America's medical knowledge with the world, and is reserved for trainees. J-1 visa holders are required to return to their home country for at least 2 years after completing their training. However, more than half the J-1 visa holders currently receive a waiver of the requirement to return to their home country under the current Conrad 30.

It is important for the Committee to be aware that there is growing international concern about the flow of physicians from undeveloped countries to the most developed and wealthiest English-speaking countries of the world. A recent World Health Organization (WHO) report released in April 2006 documents the major burden caused by the migration of physicians, nurses and other health professionals from the poorest, most needy countries to the more developed countries. An article and editorial in the *New England Journal of Medicine* this past winter and the WHO report strongly urge the developed countries to reduce their reliance on health professionals from under-developed countries.[4, 5]

Migration to the US, UK, Canada and Australia from the Indian Sub-Continent and Sub-Saran Africa

Regions and top countries	Sending country MDs in recipient countries	MDs in sending country	Emigration Factor
Indian Sub-Continent			
1. Sri Lanka	3,027	7,963	27.5
2. Pakistan	12,813	96,900	11.7
3. India	59,523	503,900	10.6
4. Myanmar	1,545	14,356	9.7
5. Bangladesh	1,718	32,498	5.0
6. Nepal	54	1,259	4.1
Sub-Saharan Africa			
1. Ghana	791	1,842	30.0
2. South Africa	6,993	30,740	18.5
3. Ethiopia	359	1,971	15.4
4. Uganda	195	1,175	14.2
5. Nigeria	4,053	30,885	11.6
6. Sudan	622	4,973	11.1

Source: Fitzhugh Mullan, November 2005

AAMC

[4] Mullan F. The Metrics of the Physician Brain Drain. *NEJM* 2005 353: 1810-1818.
[5] World Health Organization. *The World Health Report 2006 - Working Together for Health*. Geneva: WHO; 2006.

The Demand for Physician Services

As set forth earlier in this testimony, the demand for physician services is influenced by a number of factors including: population growth, aging of the population, public expectations, economic growth, changes in diagnosis and treatment, cost containment efforts, and other changes in organization and financing of services. However, most of these factors are difficult to forecast with confidence beyond a few years except the aging and growth of the population, both of which have major ramifications for the future demand for physician services.

The population of the U.S. is growing rapidly. According to the U.S. Census Bureau, the nation is growing by more than 25 million people every decade[6]. By 2020, the nation will be growing by almost 1% per year (0.8%), a rate which exceeds the expected rate of growth in the supply of physicians. Thus, we expect a decrease in the physician-to-population ratio at a time when the number of elderly will be increasing even more rapidly.

The number of Americans age 65 and older will double by 2030[7]. Why is this important? Because older Americans use far more physician services than their younger counterparts. In the outpatient setting, patients aged 65 and older averaged 6.3 physician visits a year compared with 2.7 per year for those under 65; in percentage terms this amounts to 133% more visits per year[8]. The elderly also account for a disproportionate share of hospitalizations, procedures, and high-intensity services. For instance, over half of intensive care unit (ICU) days are paid for by Medicare.[9]

---

[6] US Census. http://www.census.gov/ipc/www/usinterimproj/natprojtab02a.pdf Accessed May 15, 2006.
[7] US Census. http://www.census.gov/ipc/www/usinterimproj/natprojtab02a.pdf Accessed May 15, 2006.
[8] NAMCS, 1980, 1990, 2002 & 2003
[9] Pronovost PJ, et al. *JAMA* 2002; 288(17): 2151—2162.

Number of Americans Over 65 will Double Between 2000 - 2030

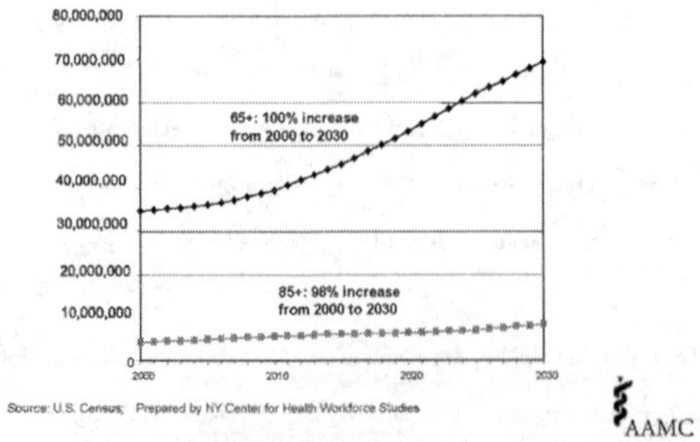

Visit Rates are Higher and Growing for Those Over 45

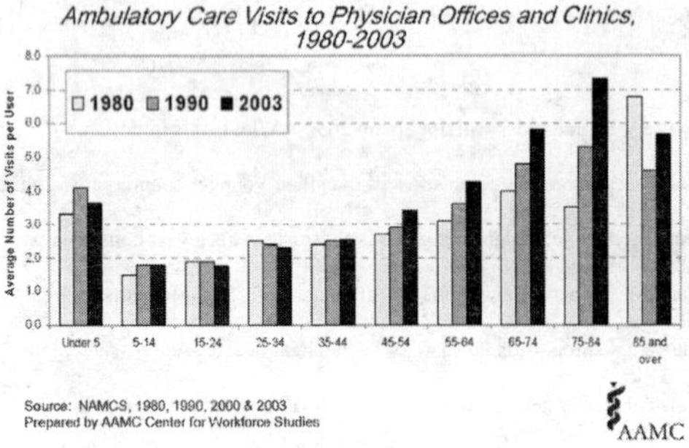

Most illnesses are also far more prevalent among the elderly. Take, for example, cancer rates: for men age 40 to 44, there are 146 new cancers per year per 100,000, while for men age 70 to 74

the rate rises to almost twenty times that of younger men at 2,806 new cases per year. If the age-specific rate of cancer is applied to Census Bureau projections of the U.S. population in 2020, the annual number of new cases will increase by nearly 50% (from 1,334,326 to 1,979,921). In fact, the incidence and prevalence of many common chronic and acute diseases will increase by similar numbers as the elderly population doubles in the next 25 years.

Age-Specific Cancer Incidence Rates/100,000, *2000*

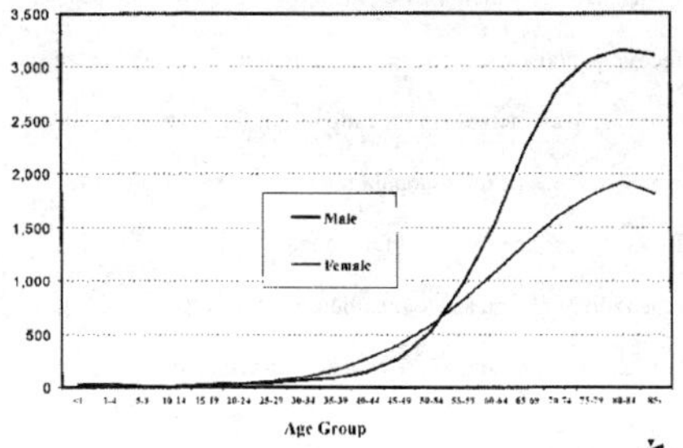

Source. CDC, Age-Specific Invasive Cancer Incidence Rates by Primary Site and Race. United Sates (U.S. Cancer Statistics, 2000).
Prepared by AAMC Center for Workforce Studies

AAMC

While new advances in treatment and early screening should bring improved outcomes, the prevalence of chronic diseases will increase over time. Patients are likely to live longer lives, but will do so with multiple conditions that require ongoing physician services and accompanying resources.

The baby-boom generation will likely expect more from the health care system than other generations before them having grown up in an era of unprecedented medical advancements. The work by Richard Cooper and others has also highlighted the positive relationship between per capita income and use of physician services which indicates that countries use more health care services as their per capita income increases (reinforcing health care as a "normal" good)[10]. Through an enormous investment in medicine, technology, and direct-to-consumer advertising, Americans have come to expect miracles from modern health care.

If current health care utilization patterns do not change, or if there are no changes in the way in which we deliver health services, the average patient in the future will consume more physician services than they do today, effectively increasing the number of physicians required to take care of the same number of people—requiring an increase in the ratio of physicians to population. Much of this increase will be related to the expanding population over the age of 65. The increase in per capita demand for health services, the declining number of hours worked by physicians, and the decrease in the ratio of physicians to population will result in a shortage of physicians in the U.S. by 2020 unless more physicians are educated and trained.

The American allopathic medical education community has spent decades developing standards and methods to help assure that schools meet appropriate requirements and that physicians that graduate from these schools have the skills and knowledge necessary to provide high quality care. The nation is better served when a greater, not lesser, proportion of future physicians are held to these standards.

Achieving the desired growth in allopathic graduates will require increased enrollment at most existing medical schools as well as the establishment of new medical schools. Increases in

[10] Cooper RA, Getzen TE, Laud P. Economic Expansion Is a Major Determinant of Physician Supply and Utilization. *Health Services Research.* April 2003;38(2):675–696.

enrollment are particularly appropriate in areas of the country where the population has grown rapidly over the past 25 years and areas where the population is projected to grow rapidly in future years. In addition, states with low medical school enrollment per capita, with numerous under-served areas, and with large and growing elderly populations may also be appropriate areas for medical school enrollment growth.

A Historical Perspective on Workforce Policies

Given the growing concern with potential shortages, some might ask why allopathic medical school enrollment hasn't increased faster. To understand this, it is important to review the history of physician workforce policy recommendations. During the 1980s and 1990s, the national Council on Graduate Medical Education (COGME), the National Academy of Science's Institute of Medicine (IOM), the Pew Health Professions Commission, the AMA, the AAMC and other national physician associations expressed strong concern with a potential surplus of physicians. The recommendations from these public and private organizations were striking in their consistency with one another.

In its 1994 report to both Congress and the Secretary of Health and Human Services, COGME concluded that, "in a managed [sic] care dominated health system, the Bureau of Health Professions projects a year 2000 shortage of 35,000 generalist physicians and a surplus of 115,000 specialist physicians" and recommended that the nation "produce 25% fewer physicians annually."[11] In 1995, the Pew Commission recommended that medical schools "by 2005 reduce the size of the entering medical school class in the U.S. by 20-25%," arguing further that this

[11] Council on Graduate Medical E. Fourth Report: Recommendation to Improve Access to Health Care Through Physician Workforce Reform. In: Services HaH, ed; 1994.

reduction should come from the closure of existing medical schools.[12] In 1996, an IOM committee recommended that "no new schools of allopathic or osteopathic medicine be opened, that class sizes in existing schools not be increased, and that public funds not be made available to open new schools or expand class size."[13] In 1996, the AAMC and five other major medical associations urged policymakers to follow IOM recommendations but also to create a national physician workforce advisory body to monitor and periodically assess the adequacy of the size and specialty composition of the physician workforce.[14]

These recommendations and analyses missed the mark for several reasons, including the incorrect belief that the nation's health care system was going to be dominated by managed care plans that would tightly control the use of services. The US population also grew more rapidly than anticipated. Finally, the studies were done in a period when the physician to population ratio was still growing from the surge in medical school enrollment in the 1960s and 70s. We are now approaching the end of this historic period of growth and it will be occurring just as the baby-boom generation begins to reach 70.

Current and Proposed AAMC Workforce Policy Recommendations

Based on the new realities, in 2005, the association issued a new position statement on the physician workforce[15]. Among the key recommendations were the following.

---

[12] Pew Health Professions C. *Critical Challenges: Revitalizing the Health Professions for the Twenty-First Century. The Third Report of the Pew Health Professions Commission* 1995.
[13] Commitee on the U.S. Physician S. *The Nation's Physician Workforce: Options for Balancing Supply and Requirements*. Washington, DC: Institute of Medicine; 1996.
[14] AAMC, AACOM, AMA, AOA, AAHC, NMA Consensus Statement on the Physician Workforce: 1996.
[15] While the association's recommendations are only recommendations, we hope that the information and logic of our recommendations encourage our members to seriously consider them. Each medical school decides on their enrollment.

1. ***The number of U.S. medical school graduates should be increased by 15% by 2015.***

In response to growing concerns about a likely future physician shortage, the association recommended that existing schools consider expanding enrollment, and that new schools be established to add an additional 2,700 graduates each year. The AAMC Executive Council is now considering a new recommendation calling for a 30% increase in allopathic medical school enrollment over the next decade compared to 2002. As indicated in the attached research brief, allopathic schools have begun to increase enrollment.

In addition to allopathic schools, osteopathic schools are also planning increases. New and existing DO schools are expected to increase enrollment by 2,000 to 3,000 per year over the next decade.

2. ***The number of graduate medical education (GME) positions reimbursed by Medicare should be increased to accommodate the increase in enrollment in U.S. medical schools.***

While U.S. medical schools have begun to respond to the growing concern about physician shortages by increasing enrollment, residency training programs also play a critical role in physician supply. In 1997, Congress established a cap on the number of resident physicians (physicians in training) that can be paid for by the Medicare program. This cap seriously discourages teaching hospitals from increasing the number of resident physicians being trained. Thus, if there is to be an adequate supply of physicians to care for Americans in the future, we will need to increase the number of GME positions supported by Medicare.

3. ***AAMC and its members remain committed to educating a diverse physician workforce***

Studies indicate that medical students from racial and ethnic minority groups are more likely to practice in under-served communities and to care for a disproportionate number of disadvantaged patients. Studies also indicate that students from rural areas are more likely to return to rural areas to practice after they complete their education. This information, coupled with other compelling arguments, undergrids the AAMC's strong advocacy for greater diversity in medical education.

4. ***The National Health Service Corps (NHSC) has played an important role in expanding access for under-served populations, and continued expansion of this program is strongly recommended.***

The NHSC is an HHS sponsored program that helps place physicians and other health care providers in communities where they are most needed, both through scholarships and through loan repayment. The NHSC has a proven record of serving the under-served in both rural and urban settings; 60% of its clinicians are located in rural areas, while the remainder serve urban populations in such settings as Community Health Centers (CHC), health departments, and other critical access facilities. A recent report in the *Journal of the American Medical Association* by Rosenblatt and colleagues demonstrates the reliance of Community Health Centers on NHSC scholars and loan repayment recipients and the inability of these safety net sites to recruit an adequate number of physicians.[16]

---

[16] Rosenblatt RA, Andrilla CHA, Curtin T, Hart LG. Shortages of Medical Personnel at Community Health Centers: Implications for Planned Expansion. *JAMA*. March 1, 2006 2006;295(9):1042-1049.

The growing debt of graduating students is likely to increase the interest and willingness of U.S. medical school graduates to apply for NHSC funding and awards. The scholarship program funds tuition and other fees for over 150 medical students annually. Moreover, almost 80% of the NHSC budget funds loan repayments for physicians that agree to serve underserved communities after the completion of residency training. The adequacy of current funding levels for loan repayments (numbering about 1,200 annually) should also be assessed to assure that they are adequate to attract physicians to the NHSC in light of growing student debt.

5. ***To assure the continuous availability of updated information on the supply and demand for physicians, the public and private sector should collectively support analysis of, and monitor changes over time in the physician workforce.***

Federal funding of medical education through programs such as Title VII has been instrumental in increasing the supply of the primary care workforce and in addressing the needs of the underserved.[17] Along with its health professions training program grants, the Bureau of Health Professions has long been the only federally funded research center studying health professions supply and demand. In addition to its own work on the nursing and physician workforce, the Bureau funded six regional centers for health workforce analysis across the nation. This small but important commitment to improving health workforce information and analysis has been eliminated from the current federal budget.

While Title VII and health workforce research have been eliminated from the 2007 budget, we have not eliminated the problems they were designed to address, including stimulating medical

[17] Meyers D, Fryer GE, Krol D, Phillips RL, Green LA, Dovey SM. Title VII funding is associated with more family physicians and more physicians serving the underserved. Am Fam Physician 2002;66:554.

school growth, increasing minority student enrollments, improving access to care for the underserved, or better understanding and planning for the future health care needs of the nation. Funding for the national Council on Graduate Medical Education (COGME) has also been eliminated. As a result of all of these changes there is little or no national leadership in physician workforce research and planning from the federal government.

The Response of Allopathic Medical Schools to the Calls for Increased Enrollment

The AAMC is making every effort to inform the medical education community about the growing likelihood of a physician shortage but does not control the number of medical student enrollments or training positions available. The AAMC's recommendation to increase enrollment has not gone unnoticed. For the 2005-06 school year, enrollment topped 17,000, a 2.1% increase from the previous year. According to a 2005 survey of medical school deans, over 40% of the nation's medical schools are likely to increase enrollment in the next five years.

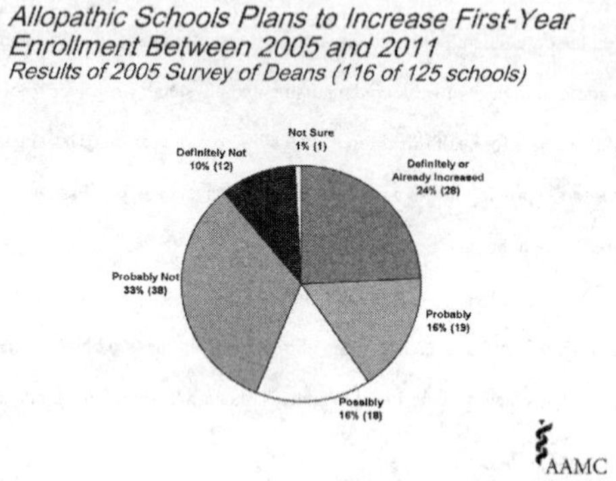

In the 2005 survey of medical school deans, 25 indicated they had "definite" plans to increase enrollments. An additional 37 schools indicated they had "probable" or "possible" plans to increase their class sizes. If all of schools follow through on their "definite," "probable" or "possible" plans to increase enrollment in the next five years, 5.4% increase from today's enrollment would result. If potential enrollees from the 5 new medical schools that are likely to be able to collectively enroll an additional 360 students by the 2010-11 academic year are factored in, a maximum of a 8.6% increase above current enrollment would occur.
The cost of building new infrastructure to support increased enrollments is the major challenge. State and local governments do the majority of financing, which is supplemented by local fundraising efforts. The federal government currently does not finance the expansion of existing schools or the development new medical schools.

In conclusion, the issues surrounding the physician workforce and potential shortages are complex. The AAMC and our member institutions are committed to assuring an adequate supply of well educated physicians to ensure that the future needs of Americans are met. Thank you for the opportunity to address the Subcommittee today. I would be happy to answer any questions you may have at this time.

ATTACHMENT 1

Analysis IN BRIEF

AAMC
Tomorrow's Doctors, Tomorrow's Cures®

Volume 6, Number 2
April 2006

Association of
American Medical Colleges

An Analysis of Medical School Expansion Plans

Growing evidence indicates that the nation will face a shortage of physicians in the next one to two decades. In 2005, the AAMC recommended a 15 percent increase in the number of U.S. medical school graduates by 2015, a small increase given the near-zero growth in M.D.-granting institutions over the last two decades. A 15 percent increase in allopathic enrollment would be about equal to an additional 2,400 students per year over 2003 levels. While osteopathic enrollment and graduations have grown by nearly 300 percent over the past 25 years, their continued growth alone will not meet the needs of the nation.

To better understand and inform the expansion plans of medical schools, this "Analysis in Brief" highlights the results of a 2005 survey of U.S. allopathic medical schools conducted by the AAMC Center for Workforce Studies.[1] Of the 125 eligible schools, 116 responded (93 percent). The information provided by schools was self-reported.

Medical Schools' Plans to Change First-Year Enrollment

Sixty-two (53 percent) of the 116 schools indicated that they would "definitely," "probably," or "possibly" change first-year enrollment in the next five years. In addition, three schools reported that they had increased enrollment since 2000, though they do not plan to change enrollment in the next five years. Altogether, 65 schools (56 percent) are considering enrollment changes or have already increased enrollment since 2000 (Figure 1).

Figure 1. Distribution of Schools by Plans to Change First-Year Enrollment, 2005

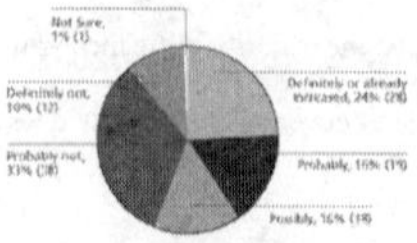

Of these schools, 28 (24 percent) reported that their plans to expand are "definite" or that enrollment had already been increased. Nineteen schools (16 percent) reported that increases are "probable" while another 18 schools (16 percent) reported "possible" expansion.

Plans to Change First-Year Enrollment by School Characteristics

The likelihood of schools to increase enrollment varied by geographic location, ownership, and other characteristics.

Region: Fifty-five percent of schools in the South and 75 percent of schools in the West reported definite or probable enrollment changes or had already increased enrollment, compared to only 16 percent of schools in the Northeast and 37 percent in the Midwest. When "possible" enrollment changes are included, two-thirds of schools in the South and over 80 percent of schools in the West are considering changing enrollment (Figure 2).

Public vs. Private: Forty-nine percent (32) of 66 public schools reported definite or probable enrollment changes or had already increased enrollment, compared with 32 percent (14) of 44

Figure 2. Schools with Plans to Change First-Year Enrollment by Region, 2005

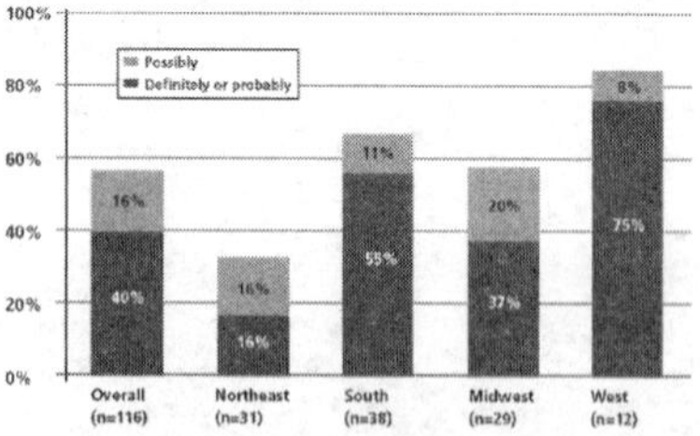

private schools responding to the survey (Figure 3). When "possible" enrollment changes are included, 64 percent of public schools and 46 percent of private schools have already increased enrollment or are considering enrollment changes.

Community-Based, Private Freestanding, and Research Intensive schools[2]: Fifty percent of community-based schools reported that they would definitely or probably change enrollment (or had already increased) compared with 31 percent of private freestanding schools and research-intensive schools. If schools with "possible" enrollment changes are included, over 80 percent of community-based schools are currently considering enrollment changes (Figure 4).

Size of Expected First-Year Enrollment

Existing U.S. allopathic medical schools expect to increase enrollment by as many as 919 first-year students by 2010-11, 5.4 percent more students than in 2005-06. Specifically:

- Of the 116 schools that responded to the survey, 25 (22 percent) indicated that they would "definitely" change enrollment over the next 5 years (by 2010-11), an increase of 453 students.
- Nineteen schools indicated "probable" enrollment changes representing 308 additional students.
- Eighteen schools indicated "possible" additional enrollment of 158 students.

It appears likely that five new allopathic schools will open in the next five years.

Figure 3. Schools with Plans to Change First-Year Enrollment by Ownership, 2005

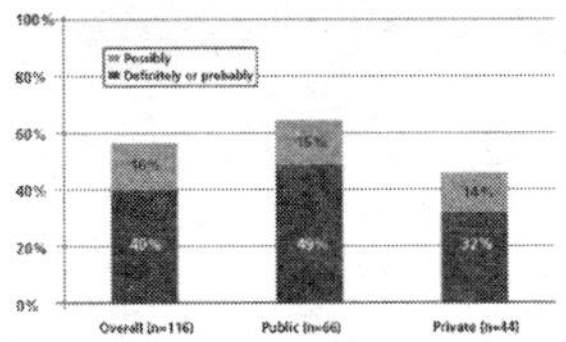

Figure 4. Schools with Plans to Change First-Year Enrollment by Institutional Type, 2005

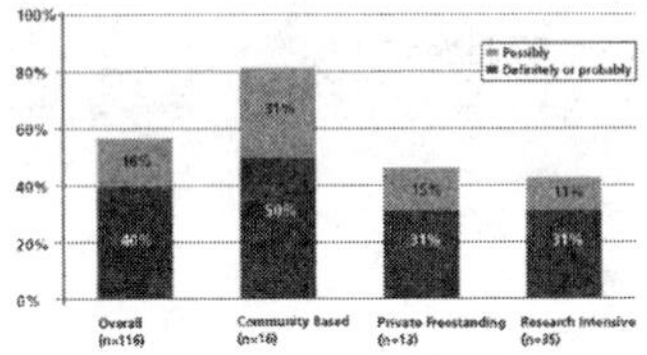

The aggregate enrollment increase from new schools is estimated to be as many as 360 students by 2010-11; by 2015, as many as 500 students per year may be enrolled in new schools.

Therefore, total annual enrollment increases from existing and new allopathic medical schools are estimated to be as many as approximately 1,400 students by 2010-11. While this represents a 9 percent growth over 2005-06 levels, or a 12.2 percent increase from 2002-03, it will not reach the 15 percent growth called for by the AAMC without additional expansion by 2015.

Conclusion

U.S. medical schools are responding to existing and expected physician shortages and the AAMC call for increased in enrollment. As of fall 2005, over 40 percent of allopathic schools are likely to increase their enrollment in the coming five years or have done so since 2000.

While current efforts are encouraging, they are unlikely to achieve the 15 percent increase recommended by the AAMC and the 3,000 graduates per year recommended by the Council on Graduate Medical Education (COGME).[3] The AAMC and COGME recommendations both are far below the likely increased demand for physician services; the fact that current plans do not even meet the current recommended increase is of concern.

Authors:
Hisashi Yamagata, Ph.D., Senior Research Associate, Center for Workforce Studies, hyamagata@aamc.org, 202-828-0236

Atul Grover, M.D., Ph.D., Associate Director, Center for Workforce Studies, agrover@aamc.org, 202-828-0666

Edward Salsberg, M.P.A, Associate Vice President and Director, Center for Workforce Studies, esalsberg@aamc.org, 202-828-0415

[1] This Analysis in Brief is excerpted from *Medical School Expansion Plans: Results of the AAMC 2005 Survey of U.S. Medical Schools*. See www.aamc.org/cfws for the full report.

[2] Private freestanding medical schools are private entities that are not part of a parent university. Community-based schools are characterized by their affiliation with community hospitals and local physicians where the schools depend upon local hospitals for clinical facilities and appoint many community physicians to their faculties. Forty research-intensive schools were selected by the volume of federal research grants and contracts awarded to support faculty work (NIH Awards to Medical Schools by Rank, Fiscal Year 2004).

[3] See www.cogme.gov/16.pdf

Association of American Medical Colleges
2450 N Street, N.W.
Washington, D.C. 20037-1127
analysis@aamc.org
www.aamc.org/data/aib

ATTACHMENT 2

AAMC
Tomorrow's Doctors, Tomorrow's Cures™

Key Physician Data by State

Association of American Medical Colleges
Center for Workforce Studies

January 2006

Version (8) Updated on 01-17-06

Association of
American Medical Colleges

Table of Contents

Figure 1.
Active Physicians per 100,000 Population, by State

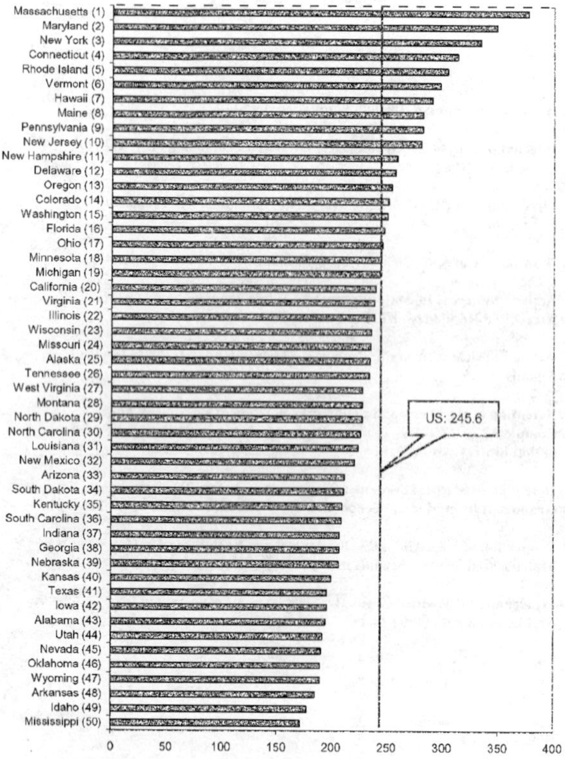

Source: AMA Masterfile, January 2005

Includes physicians who graduated from US allopathic (MD) and osteopathic (DO) schools as well as international medical graduates (IMG). Active physicians includes those involved in patient care, research, and/or administration at least 20 hours a week.

Figure 2.
International Medical Graduates (IMGs) as a Proportion of Active Physicians in the State

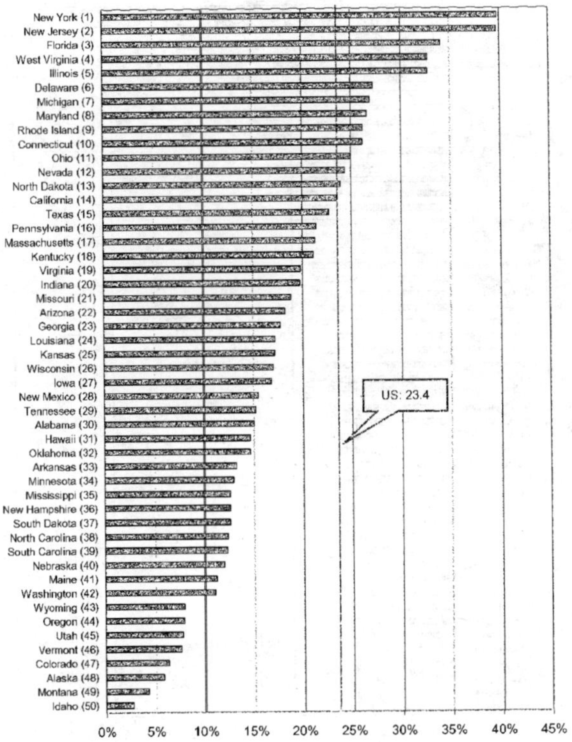

Source: AMA Masterfile, January 2005

Includes active physicians (MDs and DOs). The percentage represents active IMGs divided by total active physicians.

Figure 3.
Physicians in ACGME Residencies and Fellowships: Per 100,000 Population

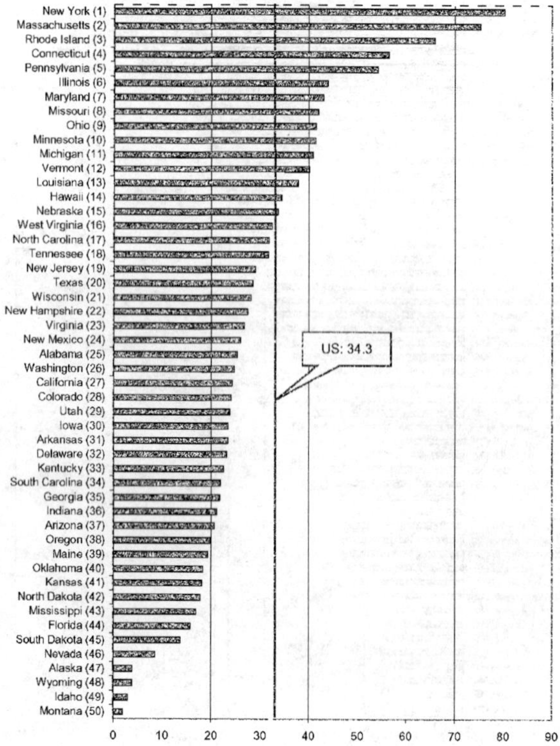

Source: AAMC GMETrack, 2004

Includes MDs, DOs, and IMGs in ACGME accredited GME training positions per 100,000 population.

Figure 4.
Number of Current Medical School Students: Per 100,000 Population

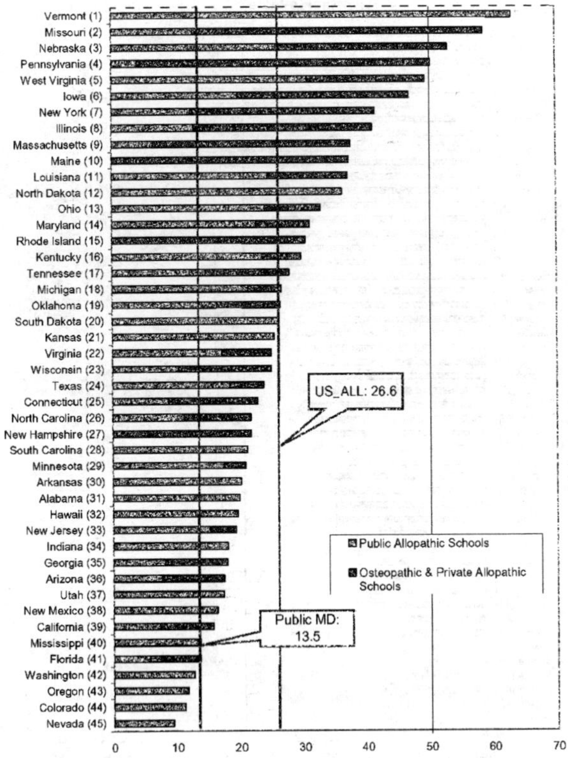

Source: AAMC FACTS Applicants, Matriculants, and Graduates

Includes students in allopathic (MD) and osteopathic (DO) schools of medicine, 2003-2004, per 100,000 population. Includes only states with a medical school located in state.

Figure 5.
Active Physicians In-State: Proportion Who Completed an ACGME Accredited Residency or Fellowship In-State

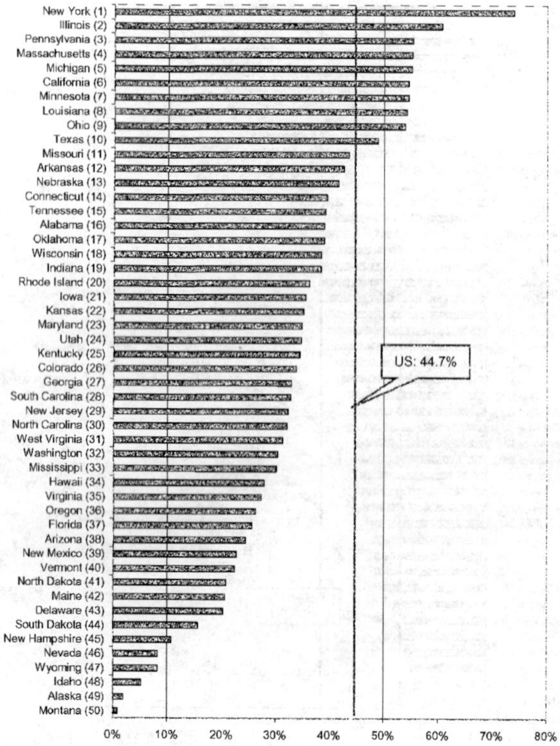

Source: AMA Masterfile, 2005

Number of active physicians in the state who completed training in-state divided by total number of active physicians in-state.

Figure 6.
Active Physicians In-State: Proportion That Attended In-State Medical Schools

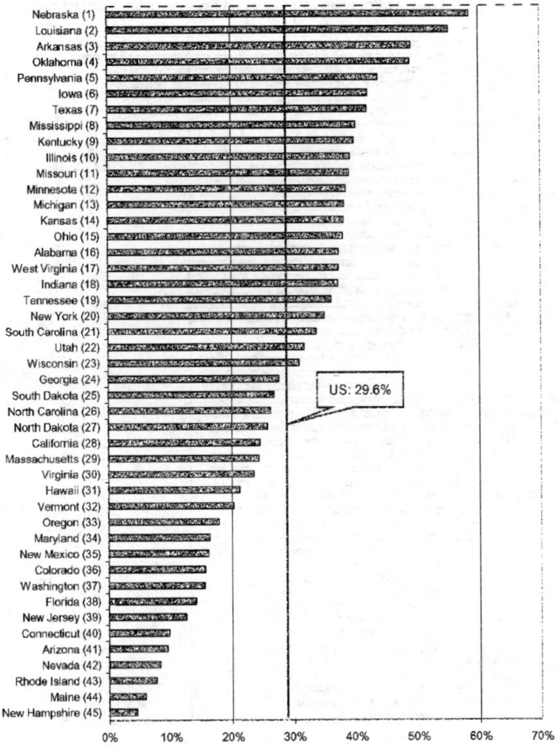

Source: AMA Masterfile, January 2005

Of the total active physicians in the state, the percentage that graduated from in-state medical schools. Includes MDs and DOs. Includes only states with a medical school located in state.

Figure 7.
Retention of Residents and Fellows: Proportion of Physicians Active in US That Completed an ACGME Training Program in a State that are Practicing in that State

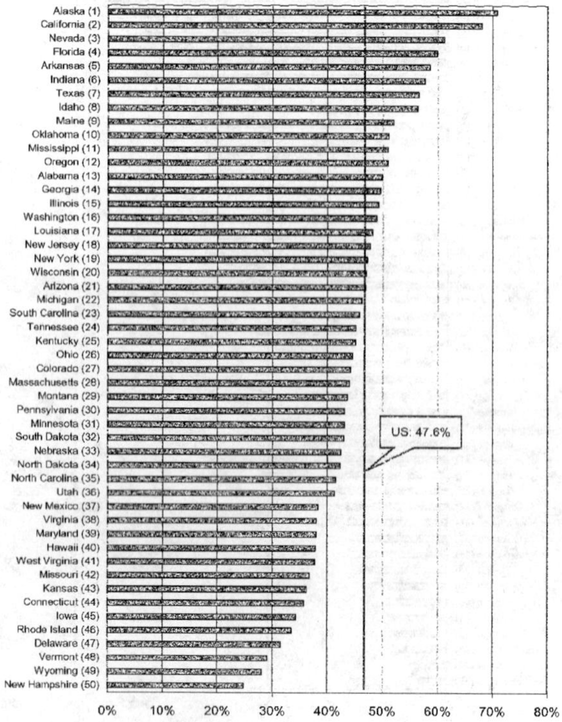

Source: AMA Masterfile, January 2005

Of the active physicians in the US who received ACGME training in a state, the percentage that are practicing in that state. Includes MDs and DOs completing ACGME accredited programs.

Figure 8.
Retention of Medical Students: Proportion of Physicians Active in US That Graduated from Medical School in a State That are Practicing in that State

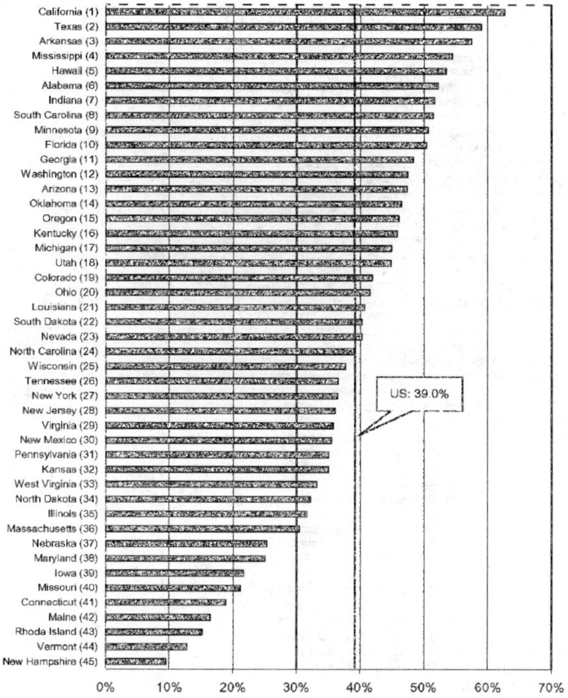

Source: AMA Masterfile, January 2005

Of active physicians in the US that went to medical school in the state, the percentage that are currently practicing in the state where they attended medical school. Includes graduates of allopathic (MD) and osteopathic (DO) schools.

Figure 9.
Proportion of New Allopathic Students from Each State That Matriculated in State Schools in 2004

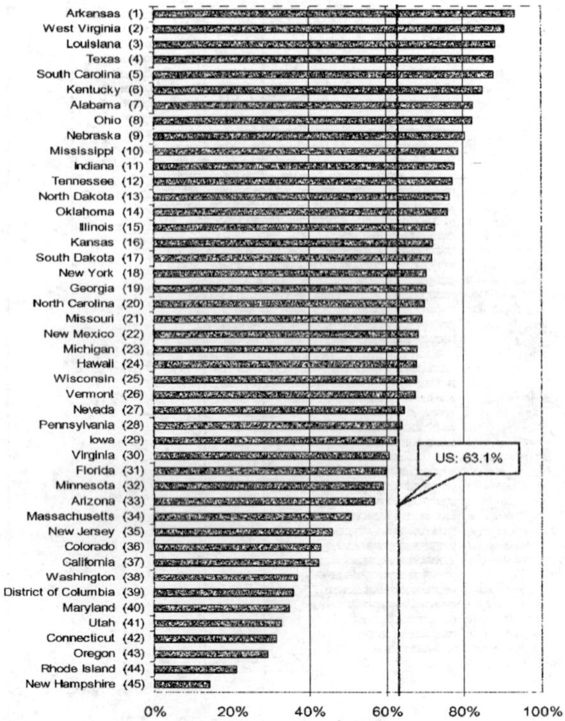

Source: *AAMC Facts*

The percentage is the number of individuals entering an allopathic medical school in the state in 2004 that listed the state as their residence divided by the total number listing the state as their residence who entered an allopathic school anywhere in the US in 2004. Overall US percentage reflects all new allopathic entrants including those from states without an allopathic school.

Figure 10.
International Medical Graduates (IMGs) as a Proportion of Residents/Fellows in ACGME Accredited Programs in the State (2004)

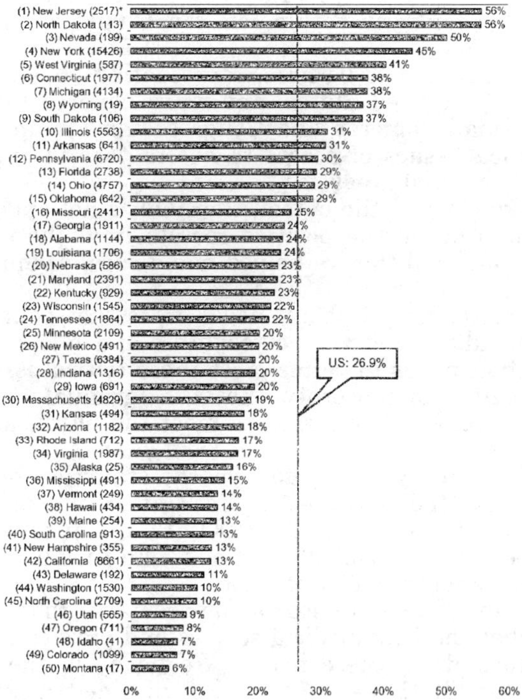

*: Number of Residents/Fellows in ACGME Accredited Programs in the State.

Source: AAMC GME Track, 2005

The percentage represents IMGs as residents/fellows in ACGME accredited programs divided by total residents and fellows in ACGME accredited programs.

Mr. HOSTETTLER. Thank you, Mr. Salsberg.
Mr. Crosby?

TESTIMONY OF JOHN B. CROSBY, J.D., EXECUTIVE DIRECTOR, THE AMERICAN OSTEOPATHIC ASSOCIATION

Mr. CROSBY. Thank you very much, Mr. Chairman and Members of the Committee.

The AOA is honored to be here, representing 56,000 osteopathic physicians in the United States, and we're honored to be working with Congressman Pomeroy and Congressman Moran on addressing these critical issues of access to health care in rural America and other underserved areas.

Let me make clear at the outset, the AOA is not opposed to H.R. 4997. We acknowledge the positive results from the J-1 visa and Conrad programs, and they've helped many rural communities over the years.

What we are concerned about, however, is that policy objectives today are not addressing U.S. osteopathic and allopathic medical schools and their needs to better meet these critical issues. Let me reiterate, the AOA is concerned that U.S. graduate medical education programs are not prepared to meet the physician workforce demands of 2020.

Right now, I'm not going to go over the statistics, but there are about 96,000 residency positions in the United States. By the year 2015, assuming there are still 24,000 PGY-1 programs around, M.D.s will need another 20,000 positions than they have today, and D.O.s will need another 5,000 positions.

Mr. Chairman, you mentioned in your remarks that you were interested in what the U.S. medical schools and physician community were doing to address these needs. We have—in the osteopathic community, since 1991, we have opened up 8 new medical schools, and we have 6 additional medical schools on the drawing board as we speak.

Since 1990, osteopathic physicians have grown in number by 67 percent. We represent 6 percent of all physicians in the United States now, 8 percent of the military, and 22 percent of all physicians practicing in rural and underserved parts of the United States.

We have 23 colleges of osteopathic medicine right now. And speaking of rural America and underserved areas, some of our newest schools have gone into Appalachia, into the rural West. We're working with Indian health centers, Eskimo populations, and others.

And our newest school is probably going to be in Harlem, New York, to meet the underserved needs of the inner city. So we're very proud of what we have done in terms of making a commitment to rural care.

There are several things you can do to address U.S. health care needs in this regard. First of all, you can assist us in helping to expand the class sizes and increase the number of new medical schools, as Dr. Salsberg and others have advocated.

You can focus more attention on training primary care physicians and general surgeons, largely through the Medicare physician payment system, which right now has a bias against those two areas of training and practice.

You can increase the training capacity in the United States. As Dr. Salsberg said, we support the AAMC in eliminating the cap from the Balanced Budget Act of 1997, which limits the number of residency training programs for U.S. trained physicians as we speak today.

You can provide financial assistance to rural hospitals who would like to start up teaching programs. Right now, it takes about 18 months before you get your first dollar from Medicare if you want to start a teaching program. Provide them a loan. Tie it to primary care. Target it to rural communities, and you can do a lot to establish new training programs here in the United States.

And again, as I said, tie it to primary care. You can improve graduate medical education training programs that foster training in rural settings, particularly nonhospital settings. Congressmen Hulshof and Talent have introduced H.R. 4403, the "Community and Rural Medical Residency Preservation Act of 2005." Your support of that legislation would go a long way.

And expanding scholarship and loan repayment programs to provide incentives for physicians practicing in rural communities would go a long way. Provide an annual tax credit equal to the amount of interest that they pay on their student loans, and also expand the current scholarship and loan repayment program to allow physicians to fulfill their commitment to rural communities on a part-time basis as well as the full-time basis currently provided by law.

We are deeply appreciative of your leadership on this critical issue. We welcome this opportunity to address these concerns. And again, we do not oppose H.R. 4997, but we think you can do a great deal to expand training for U.S. educated osteopathic and allopathic physicians.

Thank you very much.

[The prepared statement of Mr. Crosby follows:]

PREPARED STATEMENT OF JOHN B. CROSBY

Chairman Hostettler, Ranking Member Jackson Lee, and distinguished members of the Committee. My name is John Crosby. I am the executive director of the American Osteopathic Association (AOA). The AOA, which represents the nation's 56,000 osteopathic physicians and 12,000 osteopathic medical students, is honored to be here today to discuss a very important issue-access to physicians in rural and other underserved communities. We believe that by increasing training and workforce opportunities through recruitment and placement of U.S. trained osteopathic physicians you can improve access to physician services in rural communities and better address the global health needs by encouraging U.S. trained foreign medical graduates to return home to provide care to underserved populations.

We recognize that many communities face limited access to physicians and physician services. This is especially true in rural communities. We applaud the efforts made by state governments, the federal government, Members of Congress, and rural communities to increase physician access for their citizens.

For more than 130 years the AOA and the osteopathic profession have been dedicated to educating and training the future physician workforce. Consistent with our mission, we remain committed to producing primary care physicians who will practice in rural and other underserved communities. This mission has been a tenet of the profession since it's founding in the late 1800's. Today, more than sixty-five percent of all osteopathic physicians practice in a primary care specialty (family medicine, internal medicine, pediatrics, and obstetrics/gynecology). Each year, more than 65 million patient office visits are made to osteopathic physicians.

Over the past fifteen years we have enjoyed tremendous growth. Since 1990 the number of osteopathic physicians has increased sixty-seven percent. Currently, osteopathic physicians represent six percent of the total U.S. physician workforce and over eight percent of all military physicians. However, twenty-two percent of osteopathic physicians practice in a designated medically underserved area (MUA) (Map 1). Throughout our history the osteopathic profession has placed an emphasis on primary care and rural service. Our colleges of osteopathic medicine have embraced this mission. Through the years, new colleges of osteopathic medicine have been established in some of the nation's most medically underserved regions (Map 2).

The issues facing our nation's rural health care system are complex. We do not suggest that there are easy answers, but we do believe that there are policies that would increase our ability to meet these needs. The following pages outline several recommendations. These recommendations promote the ability of the AOA and our allopathic colleagues to meet the needs of rural communities without placing a greater dependence upon international medical graduates. Additionally, we believe that the implementation of these recommendations will allow the U.S. medical education system to meet its responsibilities of training international physicians who will return home and provide quality of care to their citizens. As a result of these two missions, we fulfill our joint goal of improving health care for all Americans and sharing our expertise with other countries as a means of improving global health.

INTERNATIONAL MEDICAL GRADUATES

The U.S. health care system is widely recognized as the most advanced in the world. The rapid development of new diagnoses and treatments outpaces those in other countries. We are the world's leader in medicine and medical technology. In this role, we should share our expertise with the world. For this reason, the AOA supports the continued acceptance of international medical graduates (IMGs) into the U.S. graduate medical education system. By training international physicians, we can improve the health care delivery systems around the world by improving the quality of the physicians. However, this transfer of knowledge and skills cannot take place if international physicians do not return to their home countries.

The United States should not be an importer of physicians. Physicians should come to the U.S. to train and then return home. The "brain drain" in many countries is well documented. Many countries lose their best and brightest young physicians to the United States and other English-speaking countries. The AOA believes that policies should facilitate the opposite result. International physicians should come here to train and should not be encouraged to stay upon completion of their training. In fact, we should require that they return to their home countries and practice medicine for an extended period of time before they are eligible to petition for a visa, J-1 or otherwise.

In 2006, almost 9,000 IMGs participated in the National Residency Matching Program (NRMP). Of these applicants, approximately 6,500 were not U.S. citizens and 2,500 were U.S. citizens who attended a foreign medical school. Almost fifty percent of all IMGs match to first year residency positions. In 2006, the total number of IMGs who matched to first year positions increased to 4,382.

Of the 6,500 IMG participants who were not U.S. citizens, 3,151 (48.9%) obtained first year positions. 2006 was the fifth consecutive year that the number of non-U.S. citizen IMGs matching to first year positions increased. Of the 2,500 U.S. citizen IMG participants, 1,231 (50.6%) were matched to first year positions. 2006 was the third consecutive year that the number of U.S. citizen IMGs matching to first year positions increased. The total number of IMGs filling first year residency positions will be much higher than the approximate 4,400 who secured positions through the NRMP. Many IMGs are able to secure residency training positions outside the match. All of these IMGs are allopathic physicians (MDs) and none are osteopathic physicians (DOs).

PHYSICIAN WORKFORCE

Many experts now believe that the United States will face a shortfall in its physician supply over the next twenty years. While academic and policy experts debate the needs and expectations of the future physician workforce, the AOA recognizes that we must begin to educate and train a larger cadre of physicians, now. The time it takes to educate and train a physician is, at minimum, seven years. This means that a student accepted in the matriculating class of 2006 will not enter the physician workforce until at least 2013. Due to the time required to educate and train future physicians, we believe a concentrated effort must be focused on increasing capacity over the next five years. If handled appropriately, the country could increase the physician workforce dramatically by 2020.

Reliance upon the J-1 Visa program is neither the most effective nor the most desirable way to increase physician supply in rural communities, although we recognize that the program can provide short-term relief. The J-1 program is not capable of meeting the physician workforce needs of our nation and should not be promoted for this purpose. Yes, a few states and communities have physician services as a result of the J-1 program. However, thousands of rural communities remain without physician services. The AOA supports increasing our capacity by adopting policies that encourage larger numbers of U.S. educated and trained physicians to practice in rural and underserved areas. An increase in U.S. educated and trained physicians, if properly selected and trained, will lead to a more predictable and reliable physician workforce and is more likely to produce larger numbers of physicians who will practice in rural communities.

Currently, there are 23 colleges of osteopathic medicine. Twenty of those are operating on 23 campuses. Three of those are in formation having recently received preaccreditation. In 2006, these colleges will graduate approximately 2,925 new osteopathic physicians. In 2008, the number of graduates will increase to 3,463. By 2013 the number of osteopathic physicians graduating from colleges of osteopathic medicine is projected to reach 4,706.

The AOA, like the Association of American Medical Colleges, requires maintaining of quality educational standards while class sizes are increasing. Additionally, we anticipate the establishment of at least three additional colleges of osteopathic medicine over the next four years. These new colleges, once established and accredited will begin educating approximately 500 to 600 new students each. Once fully enrolled, our current colleges, along with the new colleges of osteopathic medicine, should produce an additional 1,000 physicians per year. Assuming a predictable growth pattern, the osteopathic profession should produce approximately 5,000 new physicians per year beginning in 2015.

RECRUITMENT AND PLACEMENT

Medical schools and colleges of osteopathic medicine traditionally place significant emphasis on an applicant's academic achievement-grade point average, undergraduate degree program, and scores on the Medical College Admission Test (MCAT). While I would never suggest that the academic standards required for admittance be lowered, I do recommend that the nation's medical education institutions begin evaluating "other" factors. An evaluation of the student's life, including an evaluation of where the student was raised, attended high school, and location of family members, provides an indication of where a future physician may practice. For example, an applicant from Princeton, New Jersey is less likely to practice in a rural community than an applicant from Princeton, Indiana. If the two applicants are equally qualified, we should encourage our schools to matriculate the student from Princeton, Indiana, an individual more likely to return to rural southwest Indiana once education and training is completed.

Our medical education system must increase its efforts to promote both primary care specialties and experience in rural practice locations. Over the years, the role of the rural family physician became less glamorous than that of the urban subspecialist. Far too many medical school students want to be an "ologist" instead of a general surgeon, family physician, general internist, or pediatrician. Our nation's health care system needs specialists and subspecialists, but we need far more primary care physicians. Our medical education system must place greater emphasis on educating and training primary care physicians and general surgeons. These physicians are more likely to practice in a rural or small community hospital and are far more likely to practice in rural America.

INCREASE TRAINING CAPACITY

Currently, there are approximately 96,000 funded residency positions in the United States. Of these positions, international medical graduates fill approximately ten percent. The number of international medical graduates training in the United States has grown steadily over the past decade. The number of funded residency positions has been static since the late 1990's when Congress, as part of the Balanced Budget Act of 1997, placed a limit or "cap" on the number of residency slots any existing teaching program may have. With the exception of a provision allowing for the establishment of a rural training tract, these caps have been unaltered since their establishment.

The residency cap was established at a time when the general consensus was that the country had an adequate supply of physicians. We now recognize this is not correct. The residency caps established by the BBA limit the ability of teaching hospitals to increase training programs, thus preventing responsible growth capable of meeting our future physician workforce needs. The AOA encourages Congress to either remove or increase the cap on the number of funded graduate medical education training "slots" as established by the Balanced Budget Act of 1997.

IMPROVE RURAL TRAINING PROGRAMS

There is an old saying in medical education circles that physicians will practice within 100 miles of where they train. While the validity of this saying either in a world that is flat or alternatively in an era of globalization is unproven, its message rings true. Physicians are more likely to practice in settings where they have the most experience. While a majority of physician training takes place in the hospital setting, it should not be limited to this setting. We need to do more to expose medical students and resident physicians to different practice settings during their training years.

A valuable component of graduate medical education is the experience of training at non-hospital ambulatory sites. These sites include physician offices, nursing homes, and community health centers. Ambulatory training sites provide an important educational experience because of the broad range of patients and conditions treated and by ensuring that residents are exposed to practice settings similar to those in which they ultimately may practice. This type of training is particularly important for primary care residency programs since a majority of these physicians will practice in non-hospital ambulatory clinics upon completion of their training. This training also is essential to improving access to care in rural communities.

Congress has long recognized that a greater focus should be placed on training physicians in rural and other underserved communities. In the 1990s, Congress began to fear that the current graduate medical education payment formula discouraged the training of resident physicians in ambulatory settings. This opinion was based upon the fact that the payment formula only accounted for the resident training time in a hospital setting. Through the Balanced Budget Act of 1997, Congress altered the payment formula, removing the disincentives that existed for training in non-hospital settings. We accomplished this goal by allowing hospitals to count the training time of residents in non-hospital settings for the purpose of including such time in their Medicare cost reports for both indirect medical education (IME) and direct graduate medical education (DGME) payments.

This change in the payment formula was designed to increase the amount of training a resident physician received in non-hospital settings, enhance access to care for patients in rural and other underserved communities, provide an additional education experience for residents who are considering practicing in rural communities, and provide a recruitment mechanism for rural and underserved communities in need of physicians.

The program appeared to be working as intended. However, in 2002 the Centers for Medicare and Medicaid Services (CMS) began administratively altering the rules and regulations in respect to this issue. As a result, CMS intermediaries began denying the time residents spent in non-hospital settings. In many cases, hospitals were forced to repay thousands of dollars as a result of this administrative change in regulations. Many Members of Congress urged CMS to work with interested parties to resolve this issue by developing new regulations that clarify the appropriate use of non-hospital settings. Unfortunately, these conversations have not produced policies that meet the original intent of Congress as established in 1997. As a result, hospitals are being forced to train all residents in the hospital setting, eliminating the valuable educational experiences offered in non-hospital training sites. Additionally, some teaching hospitals may be forced to eliminate residency programs entirely as a result of current CMS policies.

Allowing hospitals to receive payments for the time resident physicians train in a non-hospital setting is sound educational policy and a worthwhile public policy goal that Congress clearly mandated in 1997. Additionally, it is good for rural communities. For this reason, the AOA encourages Congress to enact the provisions included in the "Community and Rural Medical Residency Preservation Act of 2005" (H.R. 4403).

H.R. 4403 would establish, in statute, clear and concise guidance on the use of ambulatory sites in teaching programs. If enacted, it will preserve the quality education of resident physicians originally envisioned by Congress in 1997. The Medicare program should promote quality graduate medical education, rather than impose unnecessary barriers.

The AOA also encourages Congress to establish a new grant program, operated by the Health Resource Service Administration (HRSA) that would provide "start-up" funding for rural hospitals that seek to establish new primary care residency programs. For many rural hospitals the costs associated with starting a new residency program are prohibitive. Due to CMS requirements, hospitals starting new residency programs are not eligible for funding for at least 12 months. This lag between the actual start-up date and the date of eligibility for funding is cited as one of the main reasons more hospitals, especially smaller hospitals, do not start teaching programs. The AOA believes that numerous primary care residency programs at rural hospitals could be established if financial assistance was available to offset the associated costs.

EXPAND PROGRAMS THAT PROVIDE INCENTIVES FOR RURAL PRACTICE

There are numerous existing programs that provide scholarships and loan repayment for physicians who choose to practice in rural communities. These programs include the National Health Service Corps, Public Health Service, Indian Health Service, and many programs operated by state governments. The AOA supports these programs and encourages Congress to continue funding them at levels that facilitate greater numbers of physicians practicing in rural and other underserved communities.

Additionally, we believe that some consideration should be given to allow physicians to participate in the programs on a part-time basis. There are numerous communities that need physician services, but they may not need them full time. We believe that modifications should be made to federal loan repayment and scholarship programs that allow participants to repay on a part-time basis in exchange for a longer term of service. For example, if a physician participates in the National Health Service Corps and agrees to a three-year commitment in a rural community—why not allow the physician the option of committing to 4 or 5 year's service on a part-time basis. We believe this would encourage more physicians to participate in these valuable programs without jeopardizing the underlying mission.

The AOA also proposes a change in the tax code that would provide physicians practicing in designated rural communities with a tax credit equal to the amount of interest paid on their student loans for any given year that they practice in such a community, or until their loans are paid in full. Under current law, individuals may deduct up to $2,500 in interest paid on student loans from their federal income taxes. However, the income thresholds associated with this provision often prevent physicians from qualifying. Our proposal would provide a direct link between practice location and the tax credit. A physician practicing in a rural Indiana who pays $8,000 in interest on her student loans in year one would get an $8,000 tax credit for that year. The program would continue until the physicians had retired her student loan debt or when she departed the rural community. We believe that this proposal provides a direct incentive to young physicians and would assist in the recruitment and retention of physicians in rural communities.

IMPROVE ECONOMICS OF MEDICINE

The current practice environment physicians face is challenging. Over the past decade escalating professional liability insurance premiums, decreasing reimbursements, and expanded regulations have made the practice of medicine more frustrating for all physicians. These issues are compounded in rural communities where physicians are often in solo practice or small group practices, unable to benefit from economies of scale that larger group practices in urban areas enjoy.

According to a 2004 Health Affairs study, more than half of all practicing physicians are in practices of three or fewer physicians. Three-quarters are in practices of eight or fewer. They face the same economic barriers as every other small business in America. Costs associated with staff salaries; health and other benefits, basic medical supplies, and technology, all essential components of any business, continue to rise at a rate that far outpaces reimbursements. When facing deep reductions in reimbursements at the same time that their operational costs are increasing, it is safe to project that most businesses will not be able to continue operation. While most businesses increase, or have the ability to increase, their prices to make up the differential between costs and reimbursements, physicians participating in Medicare cannot.

T3Physician Payment—Unless Congress acts, Medicare physician payment rates will be cut by 4.6 percent on January 1, 2007. If this cut is imposed, Medicare rates will fall 20 percent below the governments measure of inflation in medical practice costs from 2001–2007. If the projected cuts are implemented, the average physician payment rate will be less in 2007 than it was in 2001. Additionally, two provisions included in the Medicare Modernization Act (MMA), which provide increased reimbursements for physicians in rural communities, will expire over the next two years.

In 2002, physician payments were cut by 5.4 percent. Congress acted to avert payment cuts in 2003, 2004, 2005, and 2006 replacing projected cuts of approximately 5 percent per year with increases of 1.6 percent in 2003, 1.5 percent in 2004 and 2005, and 0 percent in 2006. Even with these increases, physician payments fell further behind medical practice costs. Practice costs from 2002 through 2005 were about two times the amount of payment increases. Since many health care programs, such as TRICARE, Medicaid, and private insurers link their payments to Medicare rates, cuts in other systems will compound the impact of the projected Medicare cuts. Medicare cuts actually trigger cuts in other programs.

Additional cuts in Medicare physician payments decrease Medicare beneficiaries' ability to access to physician services. A MedPAC survey conducted earlier this year found that 25 percent of Medicare beneficiaries reported having difficulties obtaining an appointment with a primary care physician. These problems will only increase if additional cuts are implemented. Additionally, reduced payments may prevent the implementation and adoption of new health information technologies.

Furthermore, reduced payments hamper the ability of physicians to purchase and implement new technologies in their practices. According to a 2005 study published in Health Affairs, the average costs of implementing electronic health records was $44,000 per full-time equivalent provider, with ongoing costs of $8,500 per provider per year for maintenance of the system. This is not an insignificant investment. When facing deep reductions in reimbursements, it is safe to project that physicians will be prohibited financially from adopting and implementing new technologies.

Physician payments should reflect increases in practice costs. In its 2006 March Report to Congress, the Medicare Payment Advisory Commission (MedPAC) stated that payments for physicians in 2007 should be increased 2.8 percent. Since 2001, MedPAC has recommended that the flawed SGR formula be replaced by a formula based upon increases in physician practice costs minus a productivity adjustment, which would produce annual updates equal to the Medicare Medical Economic Index (MEI).

Since its inception in 1965, a central tenet of the Medicare program is the physician-patient relationship. Medicare beneficiaries rely upon physicians for access to all other aspects of the Medicare program. This relationship has become compromised by dramatic reductions in reimbursements, increased regulatory burdens, and escalating practice costs. Given that the number of Medicare beneficiaries is expected to double to 72 million by 2030, now is the time to establish a stable, predictable, and accurate physician payment formula that reflects the cost of providing care.

Congress must act to reform the Medicare physician payment formula. Continued use of the flawed SGR formula will have a negative impact upon patient access to care. Additionally, the AOA urges Congress to approve the "Medicare Rural Health Providers Payment Extension Act" (H.R. 5118). This legislation includes provisions that extend two important rural physician payment provisions originally enacted through the MMA. H.R. 5118 extends, through 2011, a provision that provides equity in how the Medicare program views and evaluates the work of physicians regardless of geographic location. By establishing a 1.0 floor for the work geographic practice cost indices (GPCI) under the Medicare physician fee schedule, the MMA reversed years of inequities in payments between rural physicians and those in larger urban communities. The AOA was equally pleased that the MMA included a 5 percent add-on payment for physicians practicing in recognized Medicare physician scarcity areas. We believe that these are essential and positive Medicare payment policies that should be extended, if not made permanent. Both provisions will enhance beneficiary access and improve the quality of care available.

Medical Liability Reform—As you know, the nation's medical liability system is broken. In recent years physicians across the nation have faced escalating professional liability insurance premiums. According to the National Association of Insurance Commissioners (NAIC), between 1975 and 2002 medical liability premiums for physicians increased, on average, 750 percent. These premium increases are related directly to an explosion in medical liability lawsuits filed against physicians and hospitals and the rapid increase in awards. The Government Accountability Office (GAO) confirms this. In a 2003 report, the GAO stated that losses on medical liability claims are the primary driver of increases in medical liability insurance premiums.

As a result of a broken medical liability system patients face reduced access to health care, the overall costs of health care increases, and the future supply of physicians is threatened. Many physicians no longer provide services that are deemed high-risk, such as delivering babies, covering emergency departments, or performing certain surgical procedures. This crisis also impacts primary care physicians, especially those in rural areas who are often the only physician practicing in a community. As a result, patients have seen a decrease in the availability of physician services. Additionally, the medical liability crisis has a significant impact upon the career choices of future physicians. In a recent poll conducted by the AOA, eighty-two percent of osteopathic medical students stated that the cost and availability of medical liability insurance would influence their future specialty choices, while 86 percent stated that it would influence their decision on where to establish a practice once their training was complete. This trend in career choices is disturbing and will have a long-term impact upon the health care delivery system in the years ahead.

We applaud the leadership of this Committee and the House of Representatives in approving the "Help, Efficient, Accessible, Low-Cost, Timely, Health Care Act" (HEALTH Act) (H.R. 5). The AOA believes that provisions included in H.R. 5 will prove beneficial in stabilizing the nation's broken medical liability system, thus improving access to physician services.

SUMMARY

Again, the AOA appreciates the opportunity share our views on this important issue. We remain committed to working with Congress to enact legislation that will ensure access to quality physician services for all Americans, regardless of where they reside. In closing we would like to highlight five recommendations made in our testimony that we believe will lead to improved global health, increase the availability of U.S. trained physicians, improve the quality of training for future physicians, and improve the recruitment and retention of physicians in rural communities.

1. International Medical Graduates should be encouraged to return to their home countries to establish practices and, ultimately, improve the quality of care in those health care systems. The United States should not be an importer of physicians, thus contributing to the "brain drain" of other countries. By maintaining existing policy that requires IMGs to return home for two years before petitioning for a visa, we are fulfilling a noble mission of improving the health care needs of many countries.
2. Congress should consider eliminating the cap on available and funded residency positions in the U.S. This cap hinders the ability of osteopathic and allopathic medical schools to educate and train larger numbers of physicians. To meet the health care needs of our growing population we must have the capacity and financing to train a larger number of physicians.
3. Congress should enact the "Community and Rural Medical Residency Preservation Act of 2005" (H.R. 4403). This legislation would establish, in statute, clear and concise guidance on the use of ambulatory sites in graduate medical education programs. If enacted, it will preserve the quality education of resident physicians originally envisioned by Congress in 1997.
4. Congress should amend the tax code to allow physicians practicing in rural communities an annual tax credit equal to the amount of interest paid on their student loans. We believe that this proposal provides a direct incentive to young physicians and would assist in the recruitment and retention of physicians in rural communities. Additionally, Congress should revise current scholarship and loan repayment programs to allow physicians to fulfill their commitment on a part-time basis.
5. Congress should reform the Medicare physician payment formula by eliminating the sustainable growth rate and replacing it with a more equitable and predictable payment structure. Additionally, Congress should enact the "Medicare Rural Health Providers Payment Extension Act" (H.R. 5118), extending much need payment incentives for physicians practicing in rural communities.

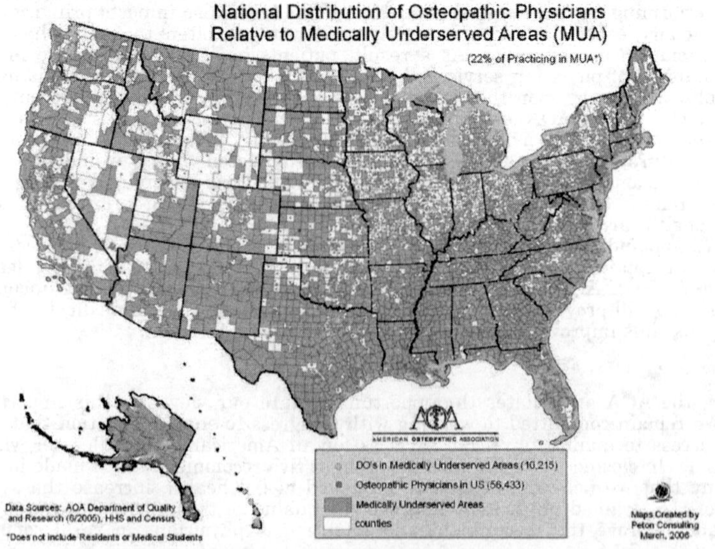

[Map 1] National Distribution of Osteopathic Physicians Relative to Medically Underserved Areas

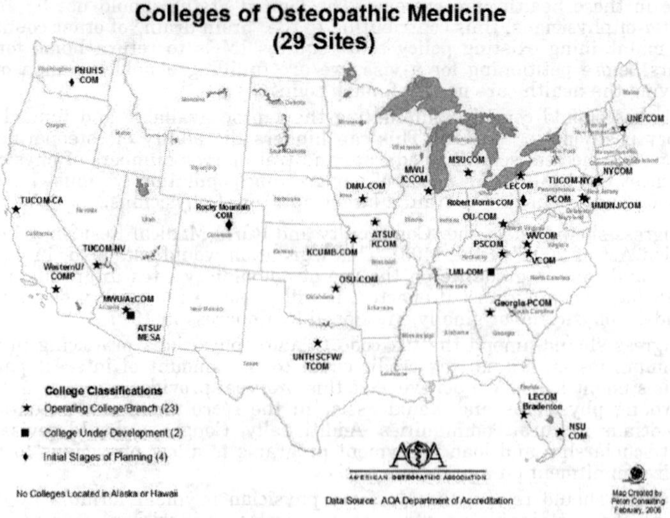

[Map 2] Colleges of Osteopathic Medicine

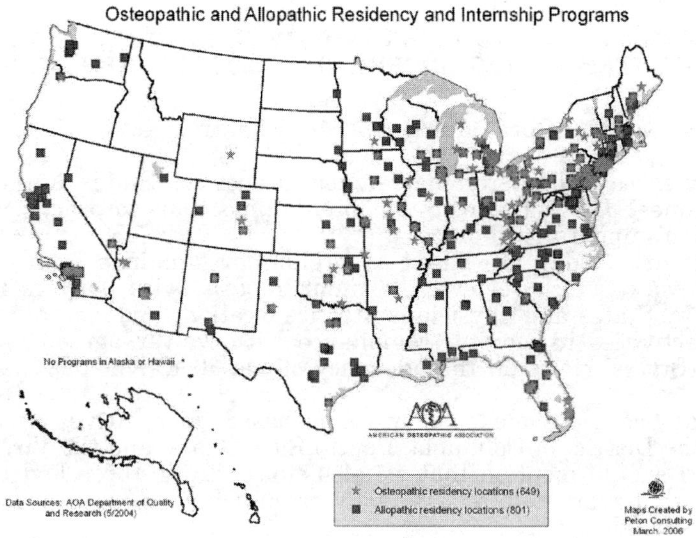

[Map 3] Osteopathic and Allopathic Residency and Internship Programs

Mr. HOSTETTLER. Thank you, Mr. Crosby.
Ms. Aronovitz?

TESTIMONY OF LESLIE G. ARONOVITZ, DIRECTOR, HEALTH CARE, UNITED STATES GOVERNMENT ACCOUNTABILITY OFFICE

Ms. ARONOVITZ. Good afternoon, Mr. Chairman and Mr. Lungren.

I am pleased to be here today as you discuss the States' authority to request J-1 visa waivers for foreign physicians to practice in the Nation's underserved areas.

My remarks today are based on preliminary findings from our ongoing work, which reviews the number of J-1 visa waivers requested by States and physicians practice locations and specialties, States' activities to monitor compliance with waiver agreements, and the States' views on the adequacy of the 30 waiver per State limit.

As Ms. Lee mentioned, our work is based on a survey of 50 States, the District of Columbia, Puerto Rico, Guam, and the Virgin Islands. I should mention that we also surveyed the three Federal agencies that requested J-1 visa waivers on behalf of States in the last few years.

In summary, we found that J-1 visa waivers remain a major means of placing physicians in underserved areas, with more than 1,000 waivers requested in each of the past 3 years for physicians to practice in nearly every State. We also found that in fiscal year 2005, States made more than 90 percent of the J-1 visa waiver requests, with the 3 Federal agencies making up the rest.

Every State, except Puerto Rico and the Virgin Islands, made requests last year, though the number varied considerably among the States. For example, about a quarter of the States requested the maximum of 30 waivers, while another quarter or a little bit over—about 29 percent of them—requested 10 or fewer waivers.

Collectively, the States requested 956 waivers, or about 60 percent of the total that were available to all the States collectively.

In terms of demographics, about 44 percent of the States' waiver requests were for physicians to practice only primary care, and about 41 percent were for physicians to practice only specialties, such as cardiology. More than three quarters of the requests were for physicians to work in hospitals or private practices.

Regarding monitoring, while States do not have an explicit responsibility for monitoring and overseeing the physicians compliance with waiver agreements, most reported conducting at least some monitoring activities. For instance, requiring periodic reports on whether the intended population in these facilities were actually being served or conducting site visits.

Regarding States' views on the 30 waiver limit, about 80 percent of the States, including many that requested close or all of the waivers—the 30 waiver limit—felt that the 30 waiver limit was adequate for their needs. However, 7 States reported that this limit was less or very much lower than what they needed.

When asked—when we asked the States if they needed more waivers, interestingly, 7—excuse me, 11 States said that they needed a total of 200 more waiver physicians. And this included 4

States that said the limit was adequate, but they still reported needing more physicians.

Regarding distribution of unused waivers, of the 44 States that did not request their 30 waiver limit—10 States did, 44 did not—25 of those 44 States said that they would be willing to have their unused waiver allotments redistributed at least either willing or willing under certain circumstances.

And for example, some of these circumstances involve their willingness if they were—if it were—it depended on the timing of the distribution. They would not want it done in the first half of the year, when there was a chance that they still might be able to attract some physicians toward the end of the year.

Others said they wanted to be sure that their needs were met before they would give up their waivers. Others advocated for a regional distribution approach, while still others mentioned possible compensation, perhaps an exchange of unused waiver allotments for more flexibility for the waivers that they did use.

Finally, several States mentioned that they would not want redistribution in 1 year to affect the number of waivers that they received to be able to ask for in another year.

In contrast to these 25 States, 14 States reported that they would not be willing to have their unused waiver allotments redistributed, and they were very concerned about the reduction in the number of physicians seeking to practice in their States. They felt that if, in fact, physicians knew that there was a redistribution program, they might wait until a more preferred location in another State cropped up before they applied for the position in a less desirable State.

What remains unclear and what we could not determine is whether any redistribution approach would simply move waiver physicians from one State to another or instead increase the overall pool of physicians seeking waivers to work in underserved areas.

I'm happy to elaborate on my findings or answer any other questions that you may have.

[The prepared statement of Ms. Aronovitz follows:]

PREPARED STATEMENT OF LESLIE G. ARONOVITZ

United States Government Accountability Office

GAO

Testimony

Before the Subcommittee on Immigration, Border Security, and Claims, Committee on the Judiciary, House of Representatives

For Release on Delivery
Expected at 2:00 p.m. EDT
Thursday, May 18, 2006

FOREIGN PHYSICIANS

Preliminary Findings on the Use of J-1 Visa Waivers to Practice in Underserved Areas

Statement of Leslie G. Aronovitz
Director, Health Care

GAO
Accountability * Integrity * Reliability

GAO-06-773T

GAO
Accountability • Integrity • Reliability

Highlights

Highlights of GAO-06-773T, a testimony before the Subcommittee on Immigration, Border Security, and Claims, Committee on the Judiciary, House of Representatives

Why GAO Did This Study

Many U.S. communities face difficulties attracting physicians to meet their health care needs. To address this problem, states and federal agencies have turned to foreign physicians who have just completed their graduate medical education in the United States under J-1 visas. Ordinarily, these physicians are required to return home after completing their education, but this requirement can be waived at the request of a state or federal agency if the physician agrees to practice in, or work at a facility that treats residents of, an underserved area. In 1996, GAO reported that J-1 visa waivers had become a major means of providing physicians for underserved areas, with over 1,300 requested in 1995. Since 2002, each state has been allotted 30 J-1 visa waivers per year, but some states have expressed interest in more.

GAO was asked to report on its preliminary findings from ongoing work on (1) the number of J-1 visa waivers requested by states and federal agencies and (2) states' views on the 30-waiver limit and on their willingness to have unused waiver allotments redistributed. Such redistribution would require legislative action.

GAO surveyed the 50 states, the District of Columbia, 3 U.S. insular areas—the 54 entities that are considered states for purposes of requesting J-1 visa waivers—and federal agencies about waivers they requested in fiscal years 2003–05.

www.gao.gov/cgi-bin/getrpt?GAO-06-773T.

To view the full product, including the scope and methodology, click on the link above. For more information, contact Leslie G. Aronovitz at (312) 220-7600 or aronovitzl@gao.gov.

May 18, 2006

FOREIGN PHYSICIANS

Preliminary Findings on the Use of J-1 Visa Waivers to Practice in Underserved Areas

What GAO Found

The use of J-1 visa waivers remains a major means of placing physicians in underserved areas of the United States. States and federal agencies reported requesting more than 1,000 waivers in each of the past 3 years. In contrast to a decade ago, states are now the primary source of waiver requests for physicians to practice in underserved areas, accounting for more than 90 percent of such waiver requests in fiscal year 2005. The number of waivers individual states requested that year, however, varied considerably. For example, about one-quarter of the states requested the maximum of 30 waivers, while slightly more than a quarter requested 10 or fewer.

Regarding the annual limit on waivers, about 80 percent of the states—including many of those that requested the annual limit or close to it—reported the 30-waiver limit to be adequate for their needs. About 13 percent reported that this limit was less than adequate. Of the 44 states that did not always request the limit, 25 reported that they would be willing to have their unused waiver allotments redistributed, at least under certain circumstances. In contrast, another 14 states reported that they would not be willing to have their unused waiver allotments redistributed. These states cited concerns such as the possibility that physicians seeking waivers would wait until a redistribution period opened and apply to practice in preferred locations in other states.

States' Requests for J-1 Visa Waivers for Physicians to Practice in Underserved Areas, Fiscal Year 2005

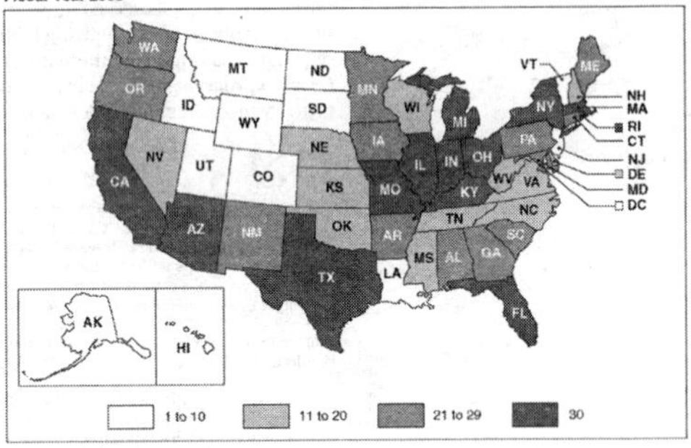

Sources: GAO survey of states (data). 2006; copyright © Corel Corp., all rights reserved (map).

Note: Guam requested two J-1 visa waivers in fiscal year 2005; Puerto Rico and the U.S. Virgin Islands requested no waivers that year.

Mr. Chairman and Members of the Subcommittee:

I am pleased to be here today as you consider the states' authority to request J-1 visa waivers for foreign physicians to practice in underserved areas[1] of the United States. As you know, many communities throughout the country—including rural and low-income urban areas—experience difficulties in attracting physicians to meet their health care needs. To address this problem, states and federal agencies have turned to foreign physicians who have just completed their graduate medical education in the United States. Many of these foreign physicians entered the United States on temporary visas, called J-1 visas, and are ordinarily required to return to their home country or country of last legal residence for 2 years when they complete their graduate medical education. This foreign residence requirement, however, can be waived by the Department of Homeland Security in certain circumstances, including at the request of a state or federal agency if the physician agrees to practice in an underserved area for at least 3 years.[2] By law, up to 30 J-1 visa waivers per year can be granted in response to each state's requests—regardless of the state's size or need for physicians.[3] There is no limit in the number of J-1 visa waivers that may be granted in response to federal agencies' requests.

In 1996, we reported that the number of J-1 visa waivers requested by states and federal agencies for physicians to work in underserved areas had risen dramatically—from 70 in 1990 to more than 1,300 in 1995—and that requesting waivers had become a major means of providing physicians for underserved areas. We estimated that, in 1995, the number of waiver physicians practicing in underserved areas exceeded the number of physicians practicing there through the National Health Service Corps (NHSC) programs—the Department of Health and Human Services' (HHS) primary mechanism for addressing shortages of physicians and other

[1]In this statement, we use the term "underserved areas" to refer to (1) areas, population groups within areas, and facilities with shortages of health care professionals or (2) areas or population groups with shortages of health care services. The Department of Health and Human Services has established specific criteria for identifying these areas, which are described in more detail later in this statement.

[2]Throughout this statement, we refer to a waiver of the 2-year foreign residence requirement as a "J-1 visa waiver" or "waiver."

[3]8 U.S.C. §§ 1182(e), 1184(l)(1)(B). States may request waivers for foreign physicians who enter the United States before June 1, 2006, under a J-1 visa for graduate medical education or who acquired such status after admission. 8 U.S.C. § 1182 note.

primary care health professionals.[4] We reported that slightly over half of these waiver physicians practiced internal medicine, and many also had medical subspecialties. Further, more than one-third of the waiver physicians practiced in nonprofit community and migrant health centers, while nearly one-fourth were in private practices. We also noted that controls for ensuring that these physicians met the terms of their waiver agreements were somewhat weak.[5] In the 10 years since our earlier report, the Department of Agriculture and the Department of Housing and Urban Development—which together requested more than 80 percent of the J-1 visa waivers for physicians in 1995—decided to stop doing so.

You and others have expressed an interest in determining how J-1 visa waivers are being used to place physicians in underserved areas. We were also asked to report on one option that has been raised as a possible means to accommodate those states that have expressed an interest in having more than 30 waivers granted at their request each year—the possibility of redistributing some states' unused waiver allotments. My remarks today are based on preliminary findings from our ongoing work and will focus on (1) the number of waivers requested by states in relation to the number requested by federal agencies; (2) practice specialties and settings of physicians whose waivers were requested by states; (3) states' activities to monitor compliance with waiver agreements; and (4) states' views on both the adequacy of the annual limit of 30 J-1 visa waivers per state and on having unused waiver allotments redistributed, which would require legislation.

To address these issues, we administered a Web-based survey to the entities eligible to request J-1 visa waivers for physicians under the authority granted to the states—the 50 states, the District of Columbia, Puerto Rico, Guam, and the U.S. Virgin Islands (hereafter referred to as "states").[6] We sent the survey to the official in each state authorized to sign

[4] NHSC places physicians and other health care professionals who are U.S. citizens or U.S. nationals in underserved areas primarily through its scholarship and educational loan repayment programs. Participating students and health professionals are required to practice in underserved areas for at least 2 years.

[5] See GAO, *Foreign Physicians: Exchange Visitor Program Becoming Major Route to Practicing in U.S. Underserved Areas*, GAO/HEHS-97-26 (Washington, D.C.: Dec. 30, 1996), and "Related GAO Products" at the end of this statement.

[6] 8 U.S.C. §1101(a)(36). We also sent a mail survey to the three federal agencies that requested waivers for physicians to practice in underserved areas in fiscal years 2003 through 2005. These included the Appalachian Regional Commission, the Delta Regional Authority, and the Department of Health and Human Services.

waiver requests or to his or her designee. The survey asked for information on states' J-1 visa waiver requests[7] for fiscal years 2003 through 2005 and on their views on the adequacy of the 30-waiver limit and having their unused waiver allotments redistributed.[8] We received a 100 percent response rate. We reviewed the surveys for internal consistency and followed up with respondents to resolve discrepancies and clarify responses; however, we did not verify the accuracy of the responses. We also reviewed relevant laws, regulations, and documents, and interviewed officials involved in reviewing and granting waivers at the Departments of State and Homeland Security. We also interviewed officials at HHS and the Educational Commission for Foreign Medical Graduates—the private, nonprofit organization that sponsors foreign physicians as exchange visitors for graduate medical education. We shared facts included in this statement with officials at the Department of State, the Department of Homeland Security, and HHS and made changes as appropriate. We conducted our work from August 2005 through May 2006 in accordance with generally accepted government auditing standards.

In summary, we found that the use of J-1 visa waivers remains a major means of placing physicians in underserved areas of the United States, with more than 1,000 waivers requested in each of the past 3 years for physicians to practice in nearly every state. In fiscal year 2005, states made more than 90 percent of these waiver requests. About 44 percent of the states' waiver requests were for physicians to practice exclusively primary care,[9] while about 41 percent were for physicians to practice exclusively nonprimary care specialties, such as anesthesiology or cardiology. Regarding practice settings, more than three-fourths of the states' waiver requests were for physicians to work in hospitals or private practices. While states do not have explicit responsibility for monitoring physicians' compliance with their waiver agreements, most states reported that they had conducted some monitoring activities, such as requiring periodic reports on patients treated and conducting site visits to the practice

[7] While comprehensive data on the number of J-1 visa waivers granted at the request of states do not exist, the federal agencies responsible for reviewing and granting state waiver requests indicated that, after review for compliance with statutory requirements and security issues, nearly all are recommended and approved.

[8] We did not ask states for their views on other options to accommodate states that would like more than 30 waivers granted at their request each year.

[9] For the purposes of this report, we define primary care to include family practice, internal medicine, obstetrics/gynecology, and pediatrics.

locations. Six states—which together accounted for about 13 percent of all state waiver requests in fiscal year 2005—reported that their states had not conducted any monitoring activities that year. Finally, regarding the states' authority to request waivers, about 80 percent of the states—including many of the states that requested the annual limit or close to it—reported the 30-waiver limit was adequate for their needs. About 13 percent, however, reported that this limit was less than adequate. Of the 44 states that did not always request the limit, 25 reported that they would be willing to have their unused waiver allotments redistributed, at least under certain circumstances, if authorized by law. In contrast, another 14 states reported that they would not be willing to have their unused waiver allotments redistributed. These states cited concerns such as the possibility that physicians seeking waivers would wait until a redistribution period opened and apply to practice in preferred locations in other states.

Background

Many foreign physicians who enter U.S. graduate medical education programs do so as participants in the Department of State's Exchange Visitor Program—an educational and cultural exchange program aimed at increasing mutual understanding between the peoples of the United States and other countries. Participants in the Exchange Visitor Program enter the United States with J-1 visas.[10] More than 6,100 foreign physicians with J-1 visas took part in U.S. graduate medical education programs during academic year 2004–05. This number was about 40 percent lower than a

[10] In addition to foreign physicians seeking to pursue graduate medical education, other categories of exchange visitors include professors and research scholars, short-term scholars, trainees, college and university students, teachers, secondary school students, specialists, international visitors, government visitors, camp counselors, au pairs, and summer work travel. *See generally* 22 C.F.R. pt. 62. Exchange visitors in these other categories are subject to the 2-year foreign residence requirement under certain circumstances. *See* 8 U.S.C. § 1182(e)(i), (ii). For more information on the Exchange Visitor Program, see GAO, *State Department: Stronger Action Needed to Improve Oversight and Assess Risks of the Summer Work Travel and Trainee Categories of the Exchange Visitor Program*, GAO-06-106 (Washington, D.C.: Oct. 14, 2005).

decade earlier, when about 10,700 foreign physicians with J-1 visas were in U.S. graduate medical education programs.[11]

Physicians participating in graduate medical education on J-1 visas are required to return to their home country or country of last legal residence for at least 2 years before they may apply for an immigrant visa, permanent residence, or certain nonimmigrant work visas.[12] They may, however, obtain a waiver of this requirement from the Department of Homeland Security at the request of a state or federal agency, if the physician has agreed to practice in, or work at a facility that treats residents of, an underserved area for at least 3 years.[13]

States were first authorized to request J-1 visa waivers on behalf of foreign physicians in October 1994.[14] Initially, states were authorized to request waivers for up to 20 physicians each fiscal year; in 2002, the annual limit was increased to 30 waivers per state.[15] Physicians who receive waivers may work in various practice settings, including federally funded health centers and private hospitals, and they may practice both primary care and

[11] The reasons for this decline are not completely understood. Foreign physicians also enter the United States for graduate medical education using other visa types, such as H-1B visas—temporary work visas for foreign nationals employed in certain specialty occupations. These other visa types may require the physician to meet additional statutory or regulatory requirements, such as evidence that the physician has a license to practice medicine in a particular state. Reliable data are not available on the extent to which these other visa types are used.

[12] 8 U.S.C. § 1182(e). Such foreign medical graduates with J-1 visas are also prohibited from changing to any other type of nonimmigrant status. 8 U.S.C. § 1258(2).

[13] 8 U.S.C. §§ 1182(e), 1184 (l)(1)(D). Physicians may also obtain a waiver at the request of the Department of Veterans Affairs (VA) if the physician has agreed to practice at a VA facility for at least 3 years. To obtain a waiver to practice in an underserved area or at a VA facility, such employment must also be determined by the Department of Homeland Security to be in the public interest. Physicians with J-1 visas may also obtain a waiver of the 2-year foreign residence requirement if the Department of Homeland Security determines that their departure from the United States would create an exceptional hardship for the physician's U.S. citizen or permanent resident spouse or child or if the return to the physician's home country or country of last residence would subject the physician to persecution because of race, religion, or political opinions.

[14] Pub. L. No. 103-416, § 220, 108 Stat. 4305, 4319. Federal agencies were first authorized to request J-1 visa waivers for physicians in graduate medical education in 1961. Pub. L. No. 87-256, § 109(c), 75 Stat. 527, 534.

[15] Pub. L. No. 107-273, § 11018(a), 116 Stat. 1758, 1825.

nonprimary care specialties.[16] States and federal agencies may impose additional limitations on their programs beyond federal statutory requirements, such as limiting the number of requests they will make for physicians to practice nonprimary care specialties.

Obtaining a J-1 visa waiver through a state request involves multiple steps. A physician must first secure a bona fide offer of employment from a health care facility that is located in, or that treats residents of, an underserved area. The physician, the prospective employer, or both then submit an application to a state to request the waiver. The state submits a request for the waiver to the Department of State. If the Department of State recommends the waiver, it forwards its recommendation to the Department of Homeland Security's U.S. Citizenship and Immigration Services (USCIS). USCIS is responsible for making the final determination and notifying the physician when a waiver is granted. According to officials involved in recommending and approving waivers at the Department of State and USCIS, after review for compliance with statutory requirements and security issues, nearly all states' waiver requests are recommended and approved. Once physicians are granted waivers, they must work at the site specified in their waiver applications for a minimum of 3 years.[17] During this period, although states do not have explicit responsibility for monitoring physicians' compliance with the terms and conditions of their waivers, states may conduct monitoring activities at their own initiative.

For purposes of J-1 visa waivers, HHS has specified two types of underserved areas in which waiver physicians may practice: health professional shortage areas (HPSAs) and medically underserved areas and populations (MUA/Ps).[18] In general, HPSAs are areas, population groups within areas, or facilities that HHS has designated as having a shortage of primary care health professionals and are identified on the basis of, among

[16]States and federal agencies requesting waivers for nonprimary care physicians are required to demonstrate a shortage of health care professionals able to provide services in that medical specialty for the patients who would be served by that physician, based on their own criteria. 8 U.S.C. § 1184(l)(1)(D)(iii).

[17]Physicians may obtain approval from USCIS to transfer to another facility or location when extenuating circumstances exist, such as when the physician's assigned facility closes.

[18]60 Fed. Reg. 48515–6 (Sept. 19, 1995).

other factors, the ratio of population to primary care physicians.[19] MUA/Ps are areas or populations that HHS has designated as having shortages of health care services and are identified using several factors in addition to the availability of primary care providers.[20] In 2004, Congress gave states the flexibility to use up to 5 of their 30 waiver allotments each year—which we call "flexible waivers"—for physicians to work in facilities that serve patients who reside in a HPSA or MUA/P, regardless of the facilities' location.[21]

No one federal agency is responsible for managing or tracking states' and federal agencies' use of J-1 visa waivers to place physicians in underserved areas. Further, no comprehensive data are available on the total number of waivers granted for physicians to practice in underserved areas. HHS's Health Resources and Services Administration is the primary federal agency responsible for improving access to health care services, both in terms of designating underserved areas and in administering programs—such as the NHSC programs—to place physicians and other providers in them. However, HHS's oversight of waiver physicians practicing in underserved areas has generally been limited to those physicians for whom HHS has requested J-1 visa waivers.

Waivers Remain a Major Means for Providing Physicians, and States Request Most Waivers

J-1 visa waivers continue to be a major means of supplying physicians to underserved areas in the United States, with states and federal agencies reporting that they requested more than 1,000 waivers in each of fiscal years 2003 through 2005. We estimated that, at the end of fiscal year 2005, the number of physicians practicing in underserved areas through the use

[19]HHS's Health Resources and Services Administration (HRSA) designates geographic areas, specific population groups within an area, or specific facilities as HPSAs. Separate designations exist for primary care and for other health care fields, such as mental health. For primary care HPSAs, designation is based in part on the basis of the ratio of population to the number of primary care physicians but may also include other factors such as health care resources available in neighboring areas. See http://bhpr.hrsa.gov/shortage/hpsacrit.htm, downloaded May 15, 2006.

[20]HRSA designates areas and populations as MUA/Ps. See http://bhpr.hrsa.gov/shortage/muaguide.htm, downloaded May 15, 2006.

[21]Pub. L. No. 108-441, § 1(d), 118 Stat. 2630.

of J-1 visa waivers was roughly one and a half times the number practicing there through NHSC programs.[22]

In contrast to our findings a decade ago, states are now the primary source of waiver requests for physicians to practice in underserved areas. In fiscal year 2005, more than 90 percent of the waiver requests for physicians were initiated by the states, compared with fewer than 10 percent in 1995.[23] (See fig. 1.) Every state except Puerto Rico and the U.S. Virgin Islands reported requesting waivers for physicians in fiscal year 2005, for a total of 956 waiver requests. In 1995—the first full year that states had authority to request waivers—nearly half of the states made a total of 89 waiver requests.

[22]Data are not available on the number of waiver physicians practicing in underserved areas at any given time. We estimated that number by totaling the number of waiver requests in each of fiscal years 2003 through 2005–which would represent the physicians expected to be fulfilling their 3-year practice period or who had waivers in process to do so. We compared that number with the number of NHSC physicians practicing in underserved areas as of September 30, 2005.

[23]In 1995, up to 20 waivers per year could be granted in response to each state's requests, so the maximum number of waivers that could be granted that year in response to the 51 states' requests was 1,080. Since 2002, the maximum number has been 50 percent higher, so the maximum number of waivers that can be granted annually in response to the 51 states' requests has been 1,620.

Figure 1: States' and Federal Agencies' Requests for J-1 Visa Waivers for Physicians

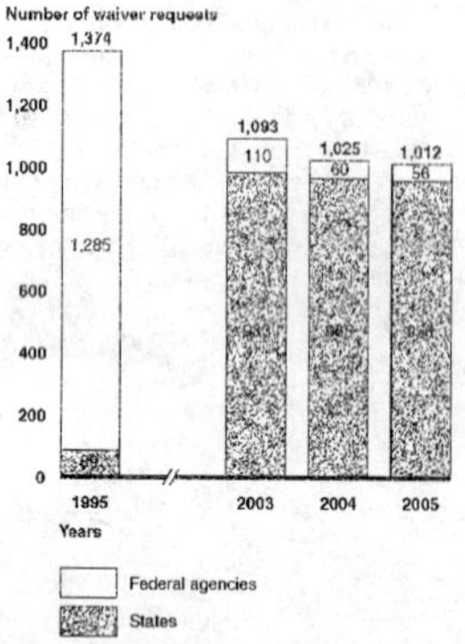

Sources: GAO/HEHS-97-26; GAO survey of states, 2005; GAO survey of federal agencies, 2005.

Note: Data apply to calendar year 1995 and fiscal years 2003 through 2005. In 1995, up to 20 waivers per year could be granted in response to each state's requests. Since 2002, the annual limit has been 30 waivers per state.

During the past decade, the two federal agencies that requested the most waivers for physicians to practice in underserved areas in 1995—the Department of Agriculture and the Department of Housing and Urban Development—have discontinued their programs.[34] These federal agencies together requested more than 1,100 waivers for physicians to practice in 47 states in 1995, providing a significant source of waiver physicians for some states. For example, these federal agencies requested a total of 149 waivers for physicians to practice in Texas, 134 for New York, and 105 for Illinois in 1995. In fiscal year 2005, the three federal agencies that requested waivers for physicians to practice in underserved areas—the Appalachian Regional Commission, the Delta Regional Authority, and

[34]The Department of Housing and Urban Development stopped requesting waivers for physicians in 1996; the Department of Agriculture stopped its program in 2002.

HHS—requested a total of 56 waivers for physicians to practice in 15 states.[25]

With diminished federal participation, states now obtain waiver physicians primarily through the 30 waivers they are allotted each year. The number of waivers states actually requested, however, varied considerably among the states in fiscal years 2003 through 2005. For example, in fiscal year 2005, about one-quarter of the states requested the maximum of 30 waivers, while slightly more than a quarter requested 10 or fewer (see fig. 2). Collectively, the 54 states requested 956 waivers, or roughly 60 percent of the maximum of 1,620 waivers that could have been granted at their request.

[25]The number of waivers requested by these agencies for physicians to practice in each of the 15 states ranged from 1 request for each of 6 states to 11 requests for Mississippi.

Figure 2: States' Requests for J-1 Visa Waivers for Physicians to Practice in Underserved Areas, Fiscal Year 2005

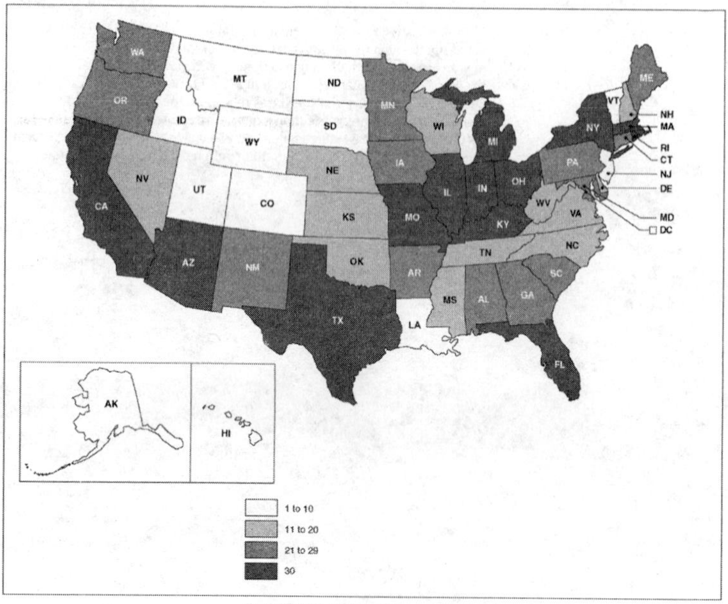

Sources: GAO survey of states (data), 2005; copyright © Corel Corp., all rights reserved (map).

Note: Guam requested two waivers in fiscal year 2005; Puerto Rico and the U.S. Virgin Islands requested no waivers that year.

States Requested Waivers for Physicians to Work in a Variety of Practice Specialties and Settings

Of the waivers states requested in fiscal year 2005, about 44 percent were for physicians to practice exclusively primary care, while about 41 percent were for physicians to practice exclusively in nonprimary care specialties, such as anesthesiology or cardiology. An additional 7 percent were for physicians to practice psychiatry.[26] A small proportion of requests (5 percent) were for physicians to practice both primary and nonprimary care—for example, for individual physicians who practice both internal medicine and cardiology (see fig. 3).

Figure 3: Specialties Practiced by Physicians for Whom States Requested J-1 Visa Waivers, Fiscal Year 2005

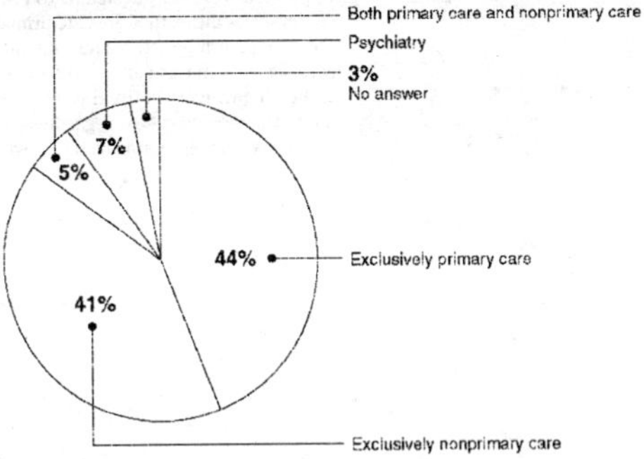

Source: GAO survey of states, 2005.

Note: Percentages are based on 956 waivers requested by 52 states in fiscal year 2005. Puerto Rico and the U.S. Virgin Islands did not request waivers that year. Psychiatry is reported as a separate medical specialty because some states' J-1 visa waiver programs have requirements for psychiatrists that differ from those for other physicians.

[26] Psychiatry is reported as a separate medical specialty because some states' J-1 visa waiver programs have requirements for psychiatrists that differ from those for other physicians. For example, a state might require psychiatrists seeking J-1 visa waivers to practice in areas that HHS has designated as mental health HPSAs.

More than 90 percent of the states that requested waivers in fiscal year 2005 reported that, under their policies in place that year, nonprimary care physicians were eligible to apply for waiver requests. Some of these states limited these requests. For example, some states restricted the number of hours a physician could practice in a nonprimary care specialty. Further, two states reported that they accepted applications from, and requested waivers for, primary care physicians only.

Regarding practice settings, more than three-fourths of the waivers requested by states in fiscal year 2005 were for physicians to practice in hospitals and private practices, including group practices. In addition, 16 percent were for physicians to practice in federally qualified health centers—facilities that provide primary care services in underserved areas—or rural health clinics—facilities that provide outpatient primary care services in rural areas (see fig. 4). More than 80 percent of the states requesting waivers in fiscal year 2005 reported requiring facilities where the physicians worked—regardless of practice setting—to accept some patients who were uninsured or covered by Medicaid.[27]

[27]Authorized under title XIX of the Social Security Act, Medicaid is the joint federal-state program that finances health care for certain low-income individuals.

Figure 4: Practice Settings of Physicians for Whom States Requested J-1 Visa Waivers, Fiscal Year 2005

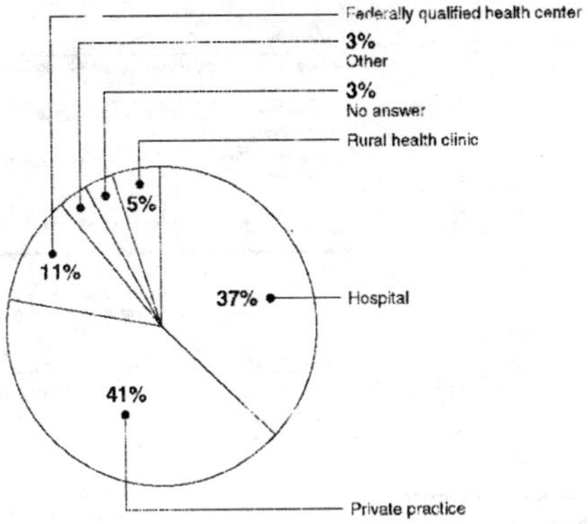

Source: GAO survey of states. 2005.

Note: Percentages are based on 956 waivers requested by 52 states in fiscal year 2005. Puerto Rico and the U.S. Virgin Islands did not request waivers that year.

Most States Reported Conducting Some Monitoring Activities

Although states do not have explicit responsibility for monitoring physicians' compliance with the terms and conditions of their waivers, in fiscal year 2005, more than 85 percent of the states reported conducting at least one monitoring activity. The most common activity—reported by 40 states—was to require periodic reports by the physician or the employer (see table 1). Some states required these reports to specify the number of hours the physician worked or the types of patients—for example, whether they were uninsured—whom the physician treated.

Table 1: Monitoring Activities States Reported Conducting in Fiscal Year 2005

Activity	Number of states conducting activity	Percentage of states conducting activity
Required periodic reports by the physician or employer	40	75
Monitored through regular communication with employers	21	40
Monitored through regular communication with physicians	19	36
Conducted periodic site visits	18	34
Other	9	17

Source: GAO survey of states, 2005.

Note: Reported activities are for the 53 states that requested any waivers in fiscal years 2003 through 2005. Puerto Rico did not request waivers during that period.

Not all states that requested waivers conducted monitoring activities. Six states, which collectively accounted for about 13 percent of all state waiver requests in fiscal year 2005, reported that they conducted no monitoring activities in that year.

Most States Reported That the Annual Limit Was Adequate but Reported Differing Views on Having Allotments Redistributed

The majority of the states reported that the annual limit of 30 waivers per state was at least adequate to meet their needs for J-1 visa waiver physicians. When asked about their needs for additional waiver physicians, however, 11 states reported needing more. Furthermore, of the 44 states that did not request their 30-waiver limit in each of fiscal years 2003 through 2005, more than half were willing, at least under certain circumstances, to have their unused waiver allotments redistributed to other states in a given year. Such redistribution would require legislation. Fourteen states reported that they would not be willing to have their states' unused waiver allotments redistributed.

Most States Reported That the Annual Waiver Limit Was Adequate, While Some Reported the Need for More

About 80 percent of the states reported that the annual limit of 30 waivers per state was adequate or more than adequate to meet their needs for J-1 visa waiver physicians. However, 13 percent of the states reported that the 30-waiver limit was less than adequate (see fig. 5).

Figure 5: States' Views on the Adequacy of the Annual Limit of 30 J-1 Visa Waivers for Physicians, 2005

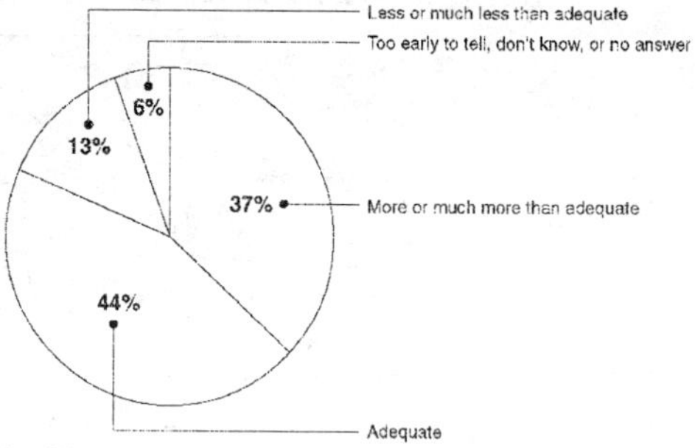

Source: GAO survey of states, 2005.

Note: Percentages are based on all 54 states eligible to request waivers.

Among the 16 states that requested 29 or 30 waivers in fiscal year 2005, 10 states reported that the annual limit was at least adequate for their needs. The other 6 states that requested all or almost all of their allotted waivers that year reported that the 30-waiver limit was less than adequate.

As mentioned earlier, states can use up to 5 of their waiver allotments for physicians to work in facilities located outside of HPSAs and MUA/Ps, as long these facilities serve patients who live in these underserved areas. While we inquired about states' views on the adequacy of the annual limit on these flexible waivers, fewer than half of the states reported requesting flexible waivers in fiscal year 2005—the first year they were authorized to do so. When asked about the annual limit of 5 flexible waivers, half of the states (27 states) reported that this limit was at least adequate, but nearly one-third (17 states) did not respond or reported that they were unsure of their need for flexible waivers. The remaining 10 states reported that the annual limit of 5 flexible waivers was less than adequate (see fig. 6). Of these 10 states, 8 had also reported that the annual limit of 30 waivers per state was at least adequate for their needs, suggesting that some states may be more interested in increasing the flexibility with which waivers may be used than in increasing the overall number of waivers each year.

Figure 6: States' Views on the Adequacy of the Annual Limit of Five Flexible J-1 Visa Waivers for Physicians to Practice Outside of HPSAs or MUA/Ps, 2005

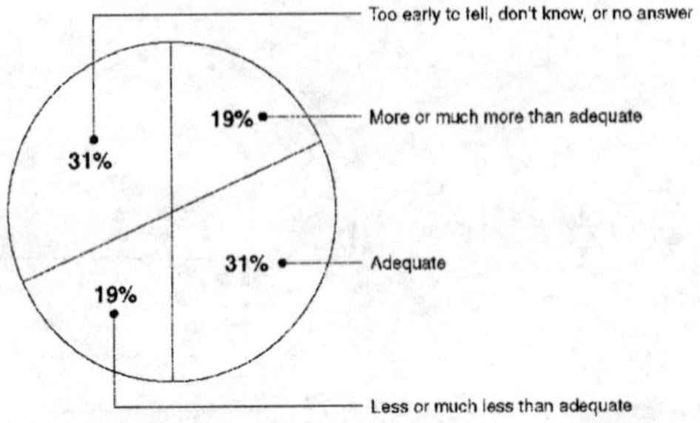

Source: GAO survey of states, 2005.

Note: Percentages are based on all 54 states eligible to request waivers.

In addition to commenting on the adequacy of the annual waiver limits, states estimated their need for additional physicians under their J-1 visa waiver programs. Specifically, 11 states (20 percent) estimated needing between 5 and 50 more waiver physicians each. Collectively, these 11 states reported needing 200 more waiver physicians (see table 2).

Table 2: Number of Additional J-1 Visa Waiver Physicians States Estimated Needing per Year, 2005

State	Estimated number of waiver physicians needed beyond annual limit of 30
Kentucky	5
Arkansas	10
Iowa	10
Louisiana	10
Massachusetts	10
West Virginia	10
California	20
Michigan	20
Arizona	25
New York	30
Texas	50
Total	**200**

Source: GAO survey of states, 2005.

Note: Data are from the 11 states that reported needing additional J-1 visa waiver physicians beyond the current annual limit of 30.

Although 10 states reported requesting the annual limit of 30 waivers in each of fiscal years 2003 through 2005, the large majority (44 states) did not. When asked to provide reasons why they did not use all 30, many of these states reported that they received fewer than 30 applications that met their requirements for physicians seeking waivers through their state J-1 visa waiver programs. Some states, however, offered further explanations, which touched upon difficulties attracting physicians to the state, low demand for waiver physicians among health care facilities or communities, and mismatches between the medical specialties communities needed and those held by the physicians seeking waivers. For example:

- *Difficulties attracting waiver physicians:* One state commented that the increase in the annual limit on waivers from 20 to 30 in 2002 opened more positions in other states, contributing to a decrease in interest among physicians seeking waivers to locate in that state. Two states suggested that because they had no graduate medical education programs or a low number of them, fewer foreign physicians were familiar with their states, affecting their ability to attract physicians seeking J-1 visa waivers.
- *Low demand for waiver physicians:* Many states noted low demand for foreign physicians among health care facilities or communities in the

states. Two of these states commented that they had relatively few problems recruiting U.S. physicians. Another state commented that health care facilities—particularly small facilities and those located in rural areas—may be reluctant to enter into the required 3-year contracts with waiver physicians because of their own budget uncertainties.

- *Lack of physicians with needed specialties:* One state commented that most communities in the state need physicians trained in family medicine and that few physicians with J-1 visas have that training. Similarly, another state noted a lack of demand among the health care facilities in the state for the types of medical specialties held by physicians seeking waivers.

In response to a question about whether they had observed any significant changes in the number of physicians seeking J-1 visa waivers, 15 states reported seeing less interest from physicians, or fewer applications, since 2001. Some states suggested that the decline might be due to an overall reduction in the number of physicians with J-1 visas who were in graduate medical education programs. Three states mentioned the possibility that more physicians may be opting to participate in graduate medical education on an H-1B visa, which does not have the same foreign residence requirement as a J-1 visa.

States' Views Differed on Having Unused Waiver Allotments Redistributed

Of the 44 states that did not use all of their waiver allotments in each of fiscal years 2003 through 2005, slightly over half (25 states) reported that they would be willing, at least under certain circumstances, to have their unused waiver allotments redistributed to other states. In contrast, about one-third of the states with unused waiver allotments (14 states) reported that they would not be willing to have their unused waiver allotments redistributed. (See table 3 and, for further details on states' responses, see app. I.)

Table 3: Views Reported by States with Unused Waiver Allotments on Their Willingness to Have Them Redistributed, 2005.

Willingness to have their unused waiver allotments redistributed	Number of states	Total number of unused waiver allotments in fiscal year 2005
Willing	11	161
Willing under certain circumstances	14	237
Not willing	14	200
No opinion	2	23
Don't know/no answer	3	43
Total	**44**	**664**

Source: GAO survey of states, 2005.

Note: Data are from the 44 states that did not request the annual limit of 30 waivers in each of fiscal years 2003 through 2005.

The 14 states that reported they would be willing under certain circumstances to have their unused waiver allotments redistributed listed a variety of conditions under which they would be willing to do so, if authorized by law. These conditions centered around the timing for redistribution, the approach for redistribution, and the possibility for compensation.

- *Timing of redistribution:* Seven states reported that their willingness to have their unused waiver allotments redistributed depended in part on when the redistribution would occur in a given year. Their comments suggested concerns about states being asked to give up unused waiver allotments before having fully determined their own needs for them. For example, three states reported that they would be willing to release at least a portion of their unused waiver allotments midway through the fiscal year. One state reported that it would be willing to have its unused waiver allotments redistributed once the state reached an optimal physician-to-population ratio. Finally, two states specified that states benefiting from any redistribution should be required to use the redistributed waivers within the same fiscal year.
- *Approach for redistribution:* Three states reported that their willingness to have their unused waiver allotments redistributed depended on how the redistribution would be accomplished. Two states reported a willingness to do so if the allotments were redistributed on a regional basis—such as among midwestern or southwestern states. Another state reported that it would be willing to have its unused waiver allotments redistributed to states with high long-term vacancy rates for physicians. This state was also

willing to have its unused waiver allotments redistributed in emergency relief situations, such as Hurricane Katrina's aftermath, to help attract physicians to devastated areas.

- *Possibility for compensation:* Two states stated that they would be willing to have their unused waiver allotments redistributed if they were somehow compensated. One state remarked that it would like more flexible waiver allotments, equal to the number of unused waiver allotments that were redistributed. The other state did not specify the form of compensation.
- *Other issues:* One state commented that it would be willing to have its unused waiver allotments redistributed as long as redistribution did not affect the number of waivers it could request in future years. Another state responded that any provision to have unused waiver allotments redistributed would need to be pilot-tested for 2 years so that its effect could be evaluated.

The 14 states that reported that they would not be willing to have their unused waiver allotments redistributed to other states cited varied concerns. Several states commented that, because of physicians' location preferences and differences in states' J-1 visa waiver program requirements, a redistribution of unused waiver allotments could possibly reduce the number of physicians seeking waivers to practice in certain states.

- *Physician location preferences:* Three states commented that physicians seeking J-1 visa waivers might wait until a redistribution period opened so that they could apply for waivers to practice in preferred states. As one state put it, if additional waivers were provided to certain states, a physician might turn down the "number 15 slot" in one state to accept the "number 40 slot" in another. This concern was also raised by four states that reported they were willing to have their unused waiver allotments redistributed under certain circumstances; two of these states specifically mentioned the possible negative impact that redistribution could have on rural areas.
- *Differences in state program requirements:* One state commented that until state requirements for waivers were made consistent among states, having unused waiver allotments redistributed would benefit states with more lenient requirements or force states with more stringent requirements to change their policies. While this state did not specify what it considered to be stringent or lenient requirements, substantial differences in state programs do exist. For example, some states restrict their waiver requests solely to primary care physicians, while others place no limits on the number of allotted waivers they request for nonprimary care physicians. In another example, four states require 4- or 5-year

contracts for all physicians or for physicians in certain specialties. One state commented that if it lost an unused waiver allotment to a state with more lenient requirements, it would have given away to another state a potential resource that it had denied its own communities.

Mr. Chairman, this concludes my prepared statement. I will be happy to answer any questions that you or Members of the Subcommittee may have.

Contact and Acknowledgments

For information regarding this testimony, please contact Leslie G. Aronovitz at (312) 220-7600 or aronovitzl@gao.gov. Contact points for our Offices of Congressional Relations and Public Affairs may be found on the last page of this statement. Kim Yamane, Assistant Director; Ellen W. Chu; Jill Hodges; Julian Klazkin; Linda Y.A. McIver; and Perry G. Parsons made key contributions to this statement.

Appendix I: State Responses to Selected Survey Questions

State	Number of waivers states reported requesting in each fiscal year			Views on adequacy of annual limit of 30 waivers	Views on adequacy of annual limit of 5 flexible waivers	Willingness to have unused waiver allotments redistributed to other states
	2003	2004	2005			
Alabama	18	19	24	Adequate	Adequate	Yes
Alaska	5	0	1	Adequate	Adequate	Yes, under certain circumstances
Arizona	30	30	30	Adequate	Adequate	[a]
Arkansas	30	30	29	Less than adequate	Don't know	Yes
California	30	30	30	Much less than adequate	No answer	[a]
Colorado	11	3	5	Much more than adequate	Much more than adequate	Don't know
Connecticut	27	30	26	More than adequate	No answer	Yes
Delaware	21	21	16	Adequate	Adequate	Yes, under certain circumstances
District of Columbia	3	9	3	More than adequate	Less than adequate	Yes
Florida	30	30	30	Adequate	No answer	[a]
Georgia	30	30	28	Adequate	More than adequate	Yes
Guam	0	1	2	Much more than adequate	Much more than adequate	Yes
Hawaii	2	1	4	More than adequate	More than adequate	Yes, under certain circumstances
Idaho	0	0	1	More than adequate	More than adequate	No
Illinois	28	30	30	Adequate	Too early to tell	No
Indiana	27	30	30	Adequate	Adequate	No
Iowa	30	30	28	Less than adequate	Too early to tell	Yes, under certain circumstances
Kansas	14	26	17	Adequate	Adequate	Yes, under certain circumstances
Kentucky	30	30	30	Adequate	Less than adequate	[a]
Louisiana	15	13	10	Too early to tell	Adequate	No
Maine	29	18	25	More than adequate	Adequate	No
Maryland	15	22	29	Adequate	Adequate	Yes, under certain circumstances
Massachusetts	28	30	30	Less than adequate	No answer	No answer
Michigan	30	30	30	Less than adequate	Less than adequate	[a]
Minnesota	30	15	21	Adequate	Too early to tell	Yes
Mississippi	19	17	18	Adequate	Less than adequate	No

State	Number of waivers states reported requesting in each fiscal year			Views on adequacy of annual limit of 30 waivers	Views on adequacy of annual limit of 5 flexible waivers	Willingness to have unused waiver allotments redistributed to other states
	2003	2004	2005			
Missouri	30	30	30	More than adequate	Much more than adequate	[a]
Montana	2	1	2	More than adequate	Adequate	Yes, under certain circumstances
Nebraska	15	7	13	Adequate	Adequate	Yes, under certain circumstances
Nevada	26	18	13	Adequate	Adequate	No
New Hampshire	6	11	15	Much more than adequate	Less than adequate	Yes, under certain circumstances
New Jersey	2	1	2	Much more than adequate	Adequate	Yes, under certain circumstances
New Mexico	29	27	29	Adequate	Adequate	Yes
New York	30	30	30	Less than adequate	Too early to tell	[a]
North Carolina	10	11	16	More than adequate	More than adequate	No
North Dakota	11	13	6	More than adequate	Much less than adequate	Yes, under certain circumstances
Ohio	30	30	30	Adequate	Much more than adequate	[a]
Oklahoma	0	17	12	More than adequate	Less than adequate	No
Oregon	20	19	22	Adequate	Too early to tell	Yes, under certain circumstances
Pennsylvania	13	16	22	More than adequate	Too early to tell	No
Puerto Rico	0	0	0	Much more than adequate	Much more than adequate	Yes
Rhode Island	30	30	30	Adequate	Too early to tell	[a]
South Carolina	30	26	21	Adequate	Adequate	No
South Dakota	10	6	6	Much more than adequate	Too early to tell	No
Tennessee	21	27	12	Adequate	Too early to tell	No
Texas	30	30	30	Much less than adequate	Adequate	[a]
Utah	4	6	5	Much more than adequate	Don't know	Yes
Vermont	0	1	2	Adequate	Less than adequate	Yes
Virgin Islands	1	0	0	Too early to tell	More than adequate	Yes, under certain circumstances
Virginia	17	13	19	No answer	Much less than adequate	No opinion
Washington	30	30	28	Adequate	Too early to tell	Yes, under certain circumstances
West Virginia	22	14	18	Adequate	Adequate	No opinion

State	Number of waivers states reported requesting in each fiscal year			Views on adequacy of annual limit of 30 waivers	Views on adequacy of annual limit of 5 flexible waivers	Willingness to have unused waiver allotments redistributed to other states
	2003	2004	2005			
Wisconsin	29	23	12	More than adequate	Too early to tell	Don't know
Wyoming	3	3	4	Much more than adequate	Much less than adequate	No

Source: GAO survey of states, 2006.

[a]States that requested 30 waivers in each of fiscal years 2003 through 2005 were not asked about their willingness to have unused waiver allotments redistributed to other states.

Related GAO Products

State Department: Stronger Action Needed to Improve Oversight and Assess Risks of the Summer Work Travel and Trainee Categories of the Exchange Visitor Program. GAO-06-106. Washington, D.C.: October 14, 2005.

Health Workforce: Ensuring Adequate Supply and Distribution Remains Challenging. GAO-01-1042T. Washington, D.C.: August 1, 2001.

Health Care Access: Programs for Underserved Populations Could Be Improved. GAO/T-HEHS-00-81. Washington, D.C.: March 23, 2000.

Foreign Physicians: Exchange Visitor Program Becoming Major Route to Practicing in U.S. Underserved Areas. GAO/HEHS-97-26. Washington, D.C.: December 30, 1996.

Health Care Shortage Areas: Designations Not a Useful Tool for Directing Resources to the Underserved. GAO/HEHS-95-200. Washington, D.C.: September 8, 1995.

GAO's Mission

The Government Accountability Office, the audit, evaluation and investigative arm of Congress, exists to support Congress in meeting its constitutional responsibilities and to help improve the performance and accountability of the federal government for the American people. GAO examines the use of public funds; evaluates federal programs and policies; and provides analyses, recommendations, and other assistance to help Congress make informed oversight, policy, and funding decisions. GAO's commitment to good government is reflected in its core values of accountability, integrity, and reliability.

Obtaining Copies of GAO Reports and Testimony

The fastest and easiest way to obtain copies of GAO documents at no cost is through GAO's Web site (www.gao.gov). Each weekday, GAO posts newly released reports, testimony, and correspondence on its Web site. To have GAO e-mail you a list of newly posted products every afternoon, go to www.gao.gov and select "Subscribe to Updates."

Order by Mail or Phone

The first copy of each printed report is free. Additional copies are $2 each. A check or money order should be made out to the Superintendent of Documents. GAO also accepts VISA and Mastercard. Orders for 100 or more copies mailed to a single address are discounted 25 percent. Orders should be sent to:

U.S. Government Accountability Office
441 G Street NW, Room LM
Washington, D.C. 20548

To order by Phone: Voice: (202) 512-6000
TDD: (202) 512-2537
Fax: (202) 512-6061

To Report Fraud, Waste, and Abuse in Federal Programs

Contact:

Web site: www.gao.gov/fraudnet/fraudnet.htm
E-mail: fraudnet@gao.gov
Automated answering system: (800) 424-5454 or (202) 512-7470

Congressional Relations

Gloria Jarmon, Managing Director, JarmonG@gao.gov (202) 512-4400
U.S. Government Accountability Office, 441 G Street NW, Room 7125
Washington, D.C. 20548

Public Affairs

Paul Anderson, Managing Director, AndersonP1@gao.gov (202) 512-4800
U.S. Government Accountability Office, 441 G Street NW, Room 7149
Washington, D.C. 20548

PRINTED ON RECYCLED PAPER

Mr. HOSTETTLER. Thank you very much, Ms. Aronovitz.

At this time, we will turn to questions from the panel. First of all, Ms. Aronovitz, you state that there has been a 40 percent decline in the past 10 years of physicians using the J-1 visa to come to the U.S. for medical training. Can this be attributed to increased usage of the H-1B visa?

Ms. ARONOVITZ. We don't really know. There are no data that really break out the physicians using H-1Bs and J-1s specifically for that comparison.

But a lot of the States who have answered our survey and other work we've done have contemplated different reasons. And one of the reasons that some States believe there is a reduction is the fact that H-1B visas are being used. So that is a valid thought on the part of very many people.

Mr. HOSTETTLER. Thank you.

Congressman Moran, as you testified, the J-1 visa has been instrumental in providing physicians to underserved areas all across your district. The National Health Services Corps, as you know, through HHS provides loan repayment for U.S. citizen health care providers who agree to work in rural areas as well as scholarships to individuals who will dedicate time of service in rural areas.

Is your experience with that program such that you believe that that could be expanded "in lieu of" the J-1 visa program? Do they complement one another? How would you——

Mr. MORAN. Mr. Chairman, I was about to answer your question "yes" until you said "in lieu of." I do think that both programs are very important. They attract, they focus on additional resources to provide health care providers, but they're two different populations. They serve the same population, but you're dealing with different applicants, different types of physicians, folks who come to the health care profession in different ways.

And so, both are very important to us. I would not at all diminish the role that the National Health Service plays in helping provide physicians, encouraging physicians to locate in underserved areas. But I don't envision, based upon even the testimony we've heard today, the number of physicians that are available from U.S. medical schools remains so tight that I think it takes both programs and even more to meet the needs of underserved areas.

So clearly not in lieu of and any way that we can expand and create a greater incentive. One of the things—we have our own State program as far as loan repayment for physicians through a State law. And many physicians have discovered that they can have their loans paid off through recruitment process if they'll locate to a more urban or suburban setting.

And so, with the loan program opportunities that are there, I think that just because more money can be made elsewhere, we're inducing a number of our physicians to—even though they have the loan program—to have their loan paid off by a community that's recruiting them to a different setting.

Mr. HOSTETTLER. Thank you.

Mr. Crosby, as you note in your testimony, one of the goals of the osteopathic profession is training primary care physicians for rural areas. How do you recruit and attract students to your colleges and specifically to serve rural areas?

And a second question would be do you believe that the J-1 visa waiver program for physicians should be expanded, as some have suggested, if not here, then elsewhere?

Mr. CROSBY. I really couldn't comment on the second question in terms of expansion of the J-1 program itself. But again, if there's a more specific question in terms of supporting that, I'd be happy to address it.

With respect to your first question, I'll just give you the example, Mr. Chairman, one of our newest schools is in Pikeville, Kentucky, the heart of Appalachia. And what they do is through the application process, try to recruit entering osteopathic medical students from the region who want to go into primary care and pledge to stay in that part of the country to practice medicine.

And about 80 percent of the students coming in want to go into primary care, and they've graduated two classes now, and 80 percent are staying in Kentucky, northern Tennessee, West Virginia, to do just that. So if you tie the application process and you screen the applicants with the right mind set, I think you can achieve those goals.

Mr. HOSTETTLER. Thank you.

Mr. Salsberg, is it fair to say that a number of qualified potential medical students are turned down each year because there is a shortage of medical school slots?

Mr. SALSBERG. Yes, we think there are many Americans who would be qualified to go to allopathic medical schools if we expand our capacity. That's one of the reasons we've recommended the expansion among our members.

Mr. HOSTETTLER. Thank you.

The Chair recognizes the gentlelady from Texas, Ms. Jackson Lee, for 5 minutes.

Ms. JACKSON LEE. I thank the Chair very much.

I think I want to be clear on the record that I do not believe the J-1 visa is a replacement for the growing need of physicians here in the United States. And I do think it's important that even beyond the jurisdiction of this Committee, that we focus the Congress on what is obviously a rising need that will reach, I think, a crisis level sometime over the next decade. And that is, of course, the need for doctors across America.

At the same time, I think that we have solutions that we can address and utilize as we speak, and so I think it's important to look at the immediacy of the problem and address it accordingly.

Congressman Moran, you've heard me make several points which I am interested in, and I will have a document to submit from the—and I ask unanimous consent to submit the statement of the National Health Care Access Coalition into the record, Mr. Chairman.

Mr. HOSTETTLER. Without objection.

Ms. JACKSON LEE. And I'll also take some quotes from this. But would you support a redistribution of the unused visa waiver shots—slots, rather?

Mr. MORAN. Well, I was interested in the testimony of the GAO. I do think, and I wouldn't want to admit that my State is one of those that would consider itself a less desirable location. But I do know that there is a fear among some States that if redistribution is allowed, that physicians are less likely to locate in what at least a physician considers to be a less desirable location for practice.

I think this is—on the other hand, I think that it's important that those States who desperately need additional physicians and—have access to those physicians. So I think there is a way——

Ms. JACKSON LEE. We have to fix it, so that we don't—we don't——

Mr. MORAN. We don't want to discourage the least—"the least desirable" locations from being——

Ms. JACKSON LEE. Allegedly. Allegedly.

Mr. MORAN. Allegedly. But we also need to recognize there is a demand in States. Texas has to be an example. It's just such a large State, that 30 in Kansas is much more beneficial than 30 in Texas.

Ms. JACKSON LEE. Absolutely. And I will cite some evidence of that. But let me also get your thoughts because this is what this Committee will have to address. The Chairman mentioned it. The movement away from J-1 visas to the H-1B visas, and do you have some thoughts on how we can legislatively address that question because it is a real concern?

Mr. MORAN. Well, I've not given a lot of thought to the H-1B visa issue. It is a competitor to this program, and the distinction is that it doesn't meet the needs of underserved areas. And so, from my perspective, we—for reasons of access to health care and reasons of health care costs—we need more physicians serving patients in the United States.

And so, I wouldn't want to take away from the physicians that come here under the H-1B. But clearly, we've got to focus the efforts at those areas of the country, urban cities and rural America, that desperately need physicians.

I think that, generally, we're going to find that the more prosperous areas of the country will be able to obtain physicians, and so the competition between the two programs I think has to be—the balance of that has to be in favor of those places that are underserved. It's a life and death issue.

Ms. JACKSON LEE. Having the Texas Medical Center near and around my congressional district and parts of it in my congressional district, the distinction is important. The J-1 visa is temporary, and I think whatever reform we do—whether it's an extension and other aspects that we need to reform, we should focus on that—that they go to underserved areas and they are immediate.

H-1B visas are individuals in on research, post docs, specialties that allow them to go to the choice areas. In fact, the medical centers and prime hospitals and others use H-1B visas to get the talented of the talented.

Not in any way to deflect on the J-1, but they are in a different category, and I think we should note that. So that we don't undermine the value that J-1 visas have, and there is that distinction that should be made.

Mr. MORAN. We can't blur that distinction because we will lose the effectiveness of the J-1 visa program.

Ms. JACKSON LEE. I agree with you. Let me ask Ms. Aronovitz. You didn't get a sense, and you're in the midst of a study, or have you——

Ms. ARONOVITZ. Yes. We have—we do have our results. We haven't analyzed them fully yet. But we do have some preliminary results.

Ms. JACKSON LEE. Then the basic—you get a sense that those who are participating or States that are participating view the J-1 visa as a positive asset to improving or assisting them in health care in their States, respective States?

Ms. ARONOVITZ. Most definitely. And as I said, most every State last year used at least one of their visa waiver slots.

Ms. JACKSON LEE. So you did not come away, though you're still analyzing, with a massive call for elimination?

Ms. ARONOVITZ. That's correct.

Ms. JACKSON LEE. Mr. Chairman, may I ask unanimous consent to put the statement—I asked that. But also—and I will quote from them, the Texas Department of State Health Services. I ask unanimous consent to put that letter in the record as well.

Mr. HOSTETTLER. Without objection.

The Chair recognizes the gentleman from California for 5 minutes. Mr. Lungren?

Mr. Daniel LUNGREN OF CALIFORNIA. Thank you very much, Mr. Chairman.

Mr. Moran, I was not in Congress when this program was first established, but it obviously was established on a temporary basis. Was that because it was to be a pilot project?

Was that because there was a thought that this need for underserved areas would be a stopgap in that somehow we were going to, through other mechanisms, provide for these underserved areas? What was the nature of the short term or sunset of it?

Mr. MORAN. Mr. Lungren, I have the same excuse that you do. I was not in Congress when the program was started, and there may be others that have the expertise at the table to answer your question.

The Conrad 20 program in 1994, I think, was an effort to give States an opportunity that they did not have, and the Federal Government's process was so slow and cumbersome for the J-1 visa program administered by Federal agencies that my guess is that Congress said let's try this. Let's see how it works. And I think the results today, 10 years later, is it is important and vital.

I also know that in the timeframe which I was here, part of the issue was related to the extension followed post 9/11, followed 9/11. And there was interest in making the program temporary so that we could determine that the necessary security risks were being evaluated by now our Department of Homeland Security to make certain that those visas that were being approved in no way were causing any threat to the national security.

So I think we've been through a series of times in which Congress wants to see how the program is working. And then, most recently, it's been let's make certain that there are no security risks involved in the program.

Mr. Daniel LUNGREN OF CALIFORNIA. In my first tenure as a Member of Congress, I recall we were dealing with the question of underserved areas at that time. And there was some question as to why these were underserved areas. I mean, we don't want to use the word "choice" areas versus "nonchoice" areas.

And one of the things that I recall being discussed at that time was that physicians like to be kept up to date in their profession. That they are assisted in doing that by being surrounded by other physicians, by quality medical staffs, by having some access to teaching hospitals, if at all possible.

And so, in some ways, people were suggesting at that time or a number of voices suggested at that time we needed stopgap measures to have doctors go for short periods of time to underserved areas, knowing they wouldn't stay there for a long time.

But there was the hope expressed that with technology in the future, that physicians might look at some of these areas as the choice areas for living purposes and that technology would allow them to fill that gap of information and reflection and exposure to colleagues and to outstanding teaching hospitals and teaching centers.

I guess my question would be to all of you on the panel, if you would give me some idea as to whether that last thought has proven to be unsuccessful or that it has, in fact, proved that we can attract more physicians to these areas that were previously underserved. And I'm talking about rural areas, as opposed to inner city right now.

And that would help me in looking at the legislation as to whether or not when we make it permanent, we're making it permanent because we think this is going to continue to be a problem forever. Or is this—have we not seen any change in terms of attracting doctors to the more rural areas in spite of the fact that they now have these technological fixes in a sense to be able to keep up with the practice, be exposed to new possibilities in medicine and so forth?

Mr. MORAN. Mr. Lungren, I can only speak from my experience, and I've worked with communities to recruit physicians. It does not seem to me that circumstances are getting any better, that the challenge is just as great as it has been in the past, and it's related to not only the issue that you suggest about the desire of collaboration with other physicians.

It's issues related to lifestyle and the sense of physicians today do not want to be on-call 7 days a week, 24 hours a day. And that's often the necessary practice in a small community. It's much easier——

Mr. Daniel LUNGREN OF CALIFORNIA. They're not going to Tuesday to Thursday schedules, are they?

Mr. MORAN. We have not gone to Tuesday to Thursday schedules. But with the arrival of advanced nurse practitioners, physician assistants, I think that's the one bright spot that I see as far as attracting and retaining physicians in rural America. We have additional assistant help.

We do have telemedicine that's available in my State. It's more now used for some consultation with experts, specialists at the University of Kansas School of Medicine. But more likely than not and perhaps unfortunately, it's used for continuing medical education for not only physicians, but nurses. It has not become a replacement for hands-on physician practice.

Mr. HOSTETTLER. The gentleman's time has expired. Without objection, the gentleman will be yielded an additional 2 minutes for the rest of the panel to respond.

Mr. CROSBY. Congressman, I think you raise a very good point. Technology offers a lot of promise in rural areas. Our own organization now provides 9 hours of credit for continuing medical education programs that doctors can get over the Internet. And their access to the latest information from the New England Journal of Medicine to a news-breaking development with pharmaceuticals or whatever is immediate access.

However, there are also I think a changing environment in terms of just lifestyle. I met—I was in Des Moines last week. I met a young doctor who had started out in Phoenix, got fed up with managed care, and has relocated to rural Iowa just because he wanted a different style of practice, which was very attractive to him.

The one thing that I don't think you can answer in terms of rural areas with technology or not is the whole sense of camaraderie, which you mentioned in your opening remarks.

Another young physician that the National Health Service Corps sent out to an island off of Alaska would see 90 patients a day, but he couldn't last more than 2 weeks without having to fly to the mainland just to see other physicians, talk to them about things that had come up in his practice, and basically cope with that emotional stress of being out there alone without anybody else to fall back on if you need it.

But technology will answer a lot of questions over time. It already is.

Ms. ARONOVITZ. One thing I can add is in our survey, we actually asked States whether they've seen an increase or a decline in interest in J-1 visa waiver physicians applying to the different States, and it was an open-ended question, and only 21 States chose to answer the question.

But of the 21, 15 States said that they've seen a definite decline in interest or in the number of applications by J-1 visa physicians or visa holders. Six States, on the other hand, said they've actually seen an increase specifically in nonprimary care areas, like specialists.

But two-thirds of the ones that answered really did see a decline, and some actually attribute it to the possibility that physicians were coming for graduate medical education on H-1Bs.

Mr. SALSBERG. You know, the problems of physician distribution have been with us for a long time and are likely to be with us for a long time. And as I mentioned earlier, I think looking at the comprehensive situation, looking at the National Health Service Corps is really the best strategy.

Relying on J-1 visa physicians, who are making an important contribution but are a shrinking number, has to be of concern as the number of underserved areas, about 20 percent of Americans live in federally designated underserved areas. So the J-1 stream is clearly not going to be a sufficient stream in looking at the whole question of how can we help address maldistribution is really what we would recommend.

Mr. HOSTETTLER. I thank the gentlemen.

The Chair will now entertain a second round of questions, and I will ask just one question in that second round. And that is of you, Ms. Aronovitz.

You note in your testimony that, in 1995, the number of waivers for foreign physicians exceeded the number of physicians participating in the National Health Service Corps that I mentioned earlier, the primary means for providing physicians to underserved areas.

Was there a decline in the usage of the NHSC, the National Health Services Corps, as a result of the increased usage of the waiver program, or does your data—can your data tell you that?

Ms. ARONOVITZ. We have—we don't have enough detailed data to really understand some of the implications. But clearly, we haven't seen that strong a relationship or that correlation. And in fact, now we see that J-1 visa waiver physicians represent about one and a half times the number of National Health Service Corps doctors that are in the field.

Mr. HOSTETTLER. Thank you. That's helpful.

The Chair recognizes the gentlelady from Texas for purposes of second round of questions.

Ms. JACKSON LEE. Thank you, Mr. Chairman, and I should be narrow in my comments.

I think the answer to your last question really has to do with what has been noted by the National Health Care Access Coalition, which is the numbers suggest that we need to expand to 200,000 doctors, and that there are currently only fewer than 800,000 doctors and that there will be a growing shortage over the next, as I indicated, couple of decades. So we're facing a shortage, and I think there have been many suggestions here that we could utilize.

Mr. Crosby, I just—what is the training of your physicians in your specialty?

Mr. CROSBY. Osteopathic physicians have the exact same training as allopathic physicians. Go to 4 years of medical school. Perhaps an internship, and then 3 or 4 or 5 years of residency training.

We deliver babies. We do neurosurgery. We provide osteopathic manipulative treatment. The whole scope of care is available through osteopathic physicians, and we're proud to have one of our medical schools in the Forth Worth/Dallas area. Sorry it's not in Houston.

Ms. JACKSON LEE. And the name of it?

Mr. CROSBY. The Texas College of Osteopathic Medicine, affiliated with the University of North Texas.

Ms. JACKSON LEE. And I think, as I listen to you, I think you even with the expanded ideas that you've offered, and I happen to support a lot of them——

Mr. CROSBY. Thank you.

Ms. JACKSON LEE [continuing]. That you still fall in a category that what you're wanting, we've got to produce more?

Mr. CROSBY. Yes.

Ms. JACKSON LEE. And you have my wholehearted support on that issue, and I'm going to be studying your testimony quite extensively because I think there can be some cross-pollenization between, though one might not think, Judiciary and the Energy and Commerce.

I think that does not speak to or speak against the immediacy of the J-1 visa, which I want to keep in a temporary framework.

And I will offer then simply, Mr. Chairman, the suggestions made by the coalition for health care access coalition—the National Health Care Access Coalition, which is recommending permanently authorize the Conrad program, increase the size of the Conrad program to 40 slots per State, and allow unused slots to be used by States that need them. And again, I think we can do so by making sure that we have the right kind of structure that it is not abused.

I then want to make note that there are six pages here of States and actual facilities that are asking for J-1 visas, and they do include the great State of Indiana and the great State of Texas.

I also want to make note of a comment from—that was written in the Denver Post, reported on a Dr. Amanpour, and the quote is that the doctor's importance is described. "He's keeping us alive. The doctor's fantastic. Without a physician, our nursing home is in jeopardy."

And one of the victims of small numbers of doctors are nursing homes. Very few and I would say competent, qualified, or either people right on the edge might not want to go in that direction, and our senior citizens need health care. And so, my question is to Dr. Salsberg.

Do you see the need of the parallel of these temporary visas for use as well as the growth that we need to do in our medical profession here in the States?

Mr. SALSBERG. Definitely. I mean, we definitely need to encourage expansion of U.S. medical schools to meet current and future medical needs. The concern on the J-1 program, as you know, was that that was a program designed to assist, as the Chairman said, less educated—assist physicians obtain education in America, training in America that could be of use to less developed parts of the world.

And so, I think we need an awareness of those concerns. And AAMC is looking at what can we do to assist other parts of the world in terms of improving their medical education and training. So it really should be a two-way street of what can we do to help them.

Ms. JACKSON LEE. Absolutely. And we hope that it is a two-way street as they come and utilize and that they take their training back to the nations, particularly developing nations.

My last point is to cite from the Texas Department of State Health Services, and just to show you the starkness of the need. Looking at specialties in 2004, there are approximately 228 physicians per 100,000 population for the United States. While in Texas, the ratio was 155 physicians per 100,000, or 30 percent below the national average.

Although we, as I said, want to reinforce the value of our home-trained physicians, we also know that the immediate need is to try to solve some of these problems and, of course, Texas has asked for 50 even above the 40 that's been recommended.

But I close by simply saying to Congressman Moran, do you feel comfortable that we can so structure the J-1 program that we answer a lot of the concerns that have been expressed here today?

Mr. MORAN. I have little doubt that if we work together as Members of Congress and with the profession, our States, that we can find a satisfactory solution. That doesn't solve the demands for physicians, but moves us in the right direction so that more people can receive adequate health care.

Ms. JACKSON LEE. I thank you, and I thank the Chairman. I think this was an important hearing. I thank the GAO for the work that they're still doing and the witnesses that were here today.

I yield back, Mr. Chairman.

Mr. HOSTETTLER. I thank the gentlelady.

I want to thank the panel of witnesses for your input and contribution to the record. It's been most helpful, and to advise Members that they have 5 legislative days to make additions to the record.

The business before the Subcommittee being completed, we are, without objection, adjourned.

[Whereupon, at 3:10 p.m., the Subcommittee was adjourned.]

APPENDIX

Material Submitted for the Hearing Record

Prepared Statement of the Honorable Sheila Jackson Lee, a Representative in Congress from the State of Texas, and Ranking Member, Subcommittee on Immigration, Border Security, and Claims

This is a legislative hearing on the Physicians for Underserved Areas Act, H.R. 4997, which was introduced by Congressman Jerry Moran on March 16, 2006. It would make the J-1 Visa Waiver Program permanent.

The J visa is used for one of the educational and cultural exchange programs. It has become a gateway for foreign medical graduates to gain admission to the United States as nonimmigrants for the purpose of graduate medical education and training. The visa most of these physicians enter under is the J-1 nonimmigrant visa.

The physicians who participate in the J-1 visa program are required to return to their home country for a period of at least two years before they can apply for another nonimmigrant visa or legal permanent resident status, unless they are granted a waiver of this requirement.

In 1994, Senator Kent Conrad established a new basis for a waiver of this requirement with an amendment to the Immigration and Nationality Act. It was known then as, "The Conrad State 20 Program." It permitted each state to obtain waivers for 20 physicians by establishing that they were needed in health professional shortage areas, known as "HPSAs."

On November 2, 2002, the Conrad 20 program was extended to 2004, and the number of waivers available to the states was increased to 30. This program, which is now referred to as the "Conrad 30"or "State 30" program, expired on June 1, 2004. On December 3, 2004, it was reinstated and extended to June 1, 2006, which is only a few weeks from now. Congressman Moran's Physicians for Underserved Areas Act would eliminate the need for future extensions by making the program permanent.

When the Conrad 30 program was established in 1994, most of those studying the supply of physicians in the United States were concerned about the distribution of physicians, as opposed to the total number of doctors being trained. It is now generally recognized that we are facing a severe physician shortage. The Health Policy Institute estimates that the shortage could grow to as much as 200,000 by 2020, an astounding possibility in view of the fact that the physician population in the United States currently is only about 800,000.

The failure to forecast this severe physician shortage may explain why from 1980 until last year no new medical schools opened in the United States. According to the Health Policy Institute, the United States needs to produce an extra 10,000 physicians per year over the next decade and a half in order to meet the demands of the country. This number assumes that the number of foreign educated physicians will remain constant.

Senator Conrad and I asked the General Accountability Office (GAO) to do a survey of state views on the Conrad 30 program. All 50 states filled out a GAO questionnaire and promptly returned it to GAO. One of the GAO investigators will testify about the results of the survey, so I will just point out a few key findings.

Approximately 80% of the states reported that the annual limit of 30 waivers per state is adequate. Only 13% reported that it is inadequate. Eleven states estimated that they need between 5 and 50 more waiver physicians, which would total 200 more waiver physicians. In FY2005, 44 states did not use all of their allotted waivers. The total of the unused waivers for that year was 664. Of these 44 states, 25 reported they were willing, or willing under certain circumstances, to have their unused waiver allotments redistributed. These states had a total of 398 unused waiver allotments in FY2005.

The J-1 visa waiver program has been in effect now for more than a decade. In addition to being a good source of additional physicians, it ensures that the additional physicians will go where they are most needed, health professional shortage areas in both rural and urban settings. I urge you therefore to support Congressman Moran's Physicians for Underserved Areas Act to make the program permanent. Thank you.

PREPARED STATEMENT OF THE HONORABLE KENT CONRAD, A U.S. SENATOR FROM THE STATE OF NORTH DAKOTA

Mr. Chairman, thank you for this opportunity to testify on the "Conrad State 30" program as you discuss its reauthorization. I appreciate your interest in addressing the physician shortage in the United States with programs such as this.

When the Conrad 20 program was enacted, approximately 85 percent of North Dakota's counties were designated, either in part or in total, as health professional shortage areas (HPSAs). The purpose of this program was to increase the supply of physicians to rural America. This very successful program has since been expanded to the Conrad State 30. It is heavily relied upon by a majority of the states, especially rural states like North Dakota.

Before the Conrad 20 program was created, North Dakota's hospitals and clinics had to use the federal J-1 visa waiver, which required a federal agency to certify the need for a physician. On one occasion, a facility in North Dakota was forced to use the Coast Guard as the interested federal agency. I was grateful that the Coast Guard, which has a small station in LaMoure, was willing to assist the local community in obtaining a needed medical professional. But relying on the Coast Guard to decide if a town in North Dakota needed a physician made no sense.

That is why I authored the Conrad State 20 program. It allows an interested State agency to make the determination that previously could only be made by a Federal agency. Not only are States more qualified to confirm health shortage areas, the program also uses HHS designated shortage areas as a baseline requirement, with the exception of five waivers that can go to physicians who will be placed in a facility that largely treats patients from HPSAs. Since 1994, this program has cut in half the number of family practice physician vacancies in North Dakota. It is critically important to rural hospitals and clinics in my state and across the country that this program be reauthorized.

However, a serious drop in Conrad State 30 applications has North Dakota hospitals deeply concerned. For instance, St. Luke's Hospital in Crosby, ND, reports that it used to have as many as 150 J-1 physician applications for an opening. Now, it has had a five-month vacancy, and only a handful of candidates have applied. Many users of the program believe the shrinking pool of J-1 visa waiver doctors is due to foreign physicians turning to H-1B visas in lieu of J-1 visas for their graduate medical education.

Like Chairman Hostettler, my constituents have noticed the disparity in how J-1 physicians in residency are treated compared to those on H-1B visas. Residents on J-1 visas must go home and contribute to their country's underserved for two years, or stay here and contribute to ours for three. But those on H-1B visas are excepted from either requirement; they are free to practice anywhere in the United States when they complete their residency programs. I believe we need to explore options to level the playing field, such as requiring residents on H1-B visas to serve three years in underserved areas.

I would also like to take this opportunity to express my strong concerns about proposals to re-distribute unused waivers from states like North Dakota to states that use all 30 of their Conrad 30 slots. With a shrinking overall pool of J-1 visa waiver doctors, any proposal to redistribute unused slots risks further reducing the number of these doctors who will apply to serve in North Dakota. In the words of Tioga Medical's President, "By allowing physicians to wait for the redistribution of slots to occur, a physician can opt to wait for states that may be more lucrative in weather conditions, culture, or other amenities." He is right. According to the Government Accountability Office, redistribution would likely benefit a handful of more populous states to the detriment of very rural states with facilities that have the most difficulty with recruitment.

The Conrad 30 program has made a very real contribution to augmenting the physician supply in rural areas that need qualified primary care physicians and specialists in critical areas of medicine such as diabetes, cardiology and orthopedic medicine, just to name a few. However, eighty-one percent of North Dakota's counties remain HPSA-designated some twelve years later. With the physician shortage in this country projected to reach 200,000 by 2020, the Conrad 30 program is needed now more than ever.

Since its inception, we have had to reauthorize this program many times—every two years since 2000. Such uncertainty is unnecessary. Our rural areas need to know they can count on this program for years to come. I urge the Committee to support the Physicians for Underserved Areas Act to permanently authorize this critical program for rural America and ask that the articles that I've included with my testimony be submitted for the record.

ATTACHMENT

Crosby Journal

Rural areas hit hard by doctor crunch

By Cecile Wehrman

A shrinking number of foreign doctors in a once popular visa program and a growing doctor shortage nationwide are taking a heavy toll on rural health care.

The number of foreign doctors applying for a J1 visa, which requires them to commit to working in underserved areas, has fallen drastically in the last few years.

Small town hospitals like those in Crosby and Tioga are being left out in the cold.

"We used to have 150 applicants," said St. Luke's Hospital Administrator Les Urvand, when advertising for J1 visa candidates.

As the hospital enters its fifth month with a vacancy, just a handful of candidates have applied.

The story is much the same in Tioga, which received a lengthy notice of the impending departure of Dr. Makesh Patel. Only four candidates have applied for the job, which will become vacant in June.

This is the first of two parts exploring the shortage of doctors in rural North Dakota.

NEXT WEEK: The cultural trade-offs for foreign physicians and the potential for legislation to close the HIB visa loophole.

Tioga and Crosby are not alone in needing to recruit a physician. Eighty-one percent of the state is in a health professional shortage area.

Since 1994, the J1 visa program has cut the number of family practice physician vacancies in half, but there remain at any time about 20 vacancies in North Dakota.

Tioga Medical Center Administrator Randall Peterson said they've offered the job to two doctors.

"Both turned us down because the spouse didn't want to move here."

That's a common problem, said Mary Amundson of the Center for Rural Health in Grand Forks. Often, these doctors have spouses who are also professionals seeking employment. Small towns can't always provide placement for both spouses.

But Peterson has found cultural differences are also a key.

"They want a town that has another Pakastani doctor to relate with," he said.

The growing emphasis on specialty practice is another detriment to small town hospitals trying to attract and keep physicians.

"It's tough because primary care is not on the radar of a lot of young people today," Amundson said. "A lot of students don't want the lifestyle of a family physician in a rural area."

Dr. Ivan Tsutskiridze of Crosby knows what that lifestyle is all about. Recruited as a second doctor for the community less than two years ago, today he is the sole physician in town. He works two weeks on call 24 hours a day, with one 36-hour break. Once every two months he gets five days off in a row.

Though he'd like to be closer to some big city conveniences, he likes the quiet and safety of Crosby.

He isn't sure why there are so few J-1 candidates, but he sees the program as a good exchange. Foreign doctors get the advanced experience they seek, and rural areas get the doctors they need.

"Otherwise, people won't come here," he said.

Sen. Kent Conrad, who helped establish the J1 program, has asked for a study of the issues.

"I'm very aware of this problem, and I've asked the Government Accountability Office to complete a report on why the pool of available J1 doctors has shrunk," Conrad said.

One issue, Conrad and Amundson believe, is the growing availability of H1B visas, which do not require doctors to serve rural or other underserved areas.

"It makes no sense to allow one visa program to undercut the original intent of the law -- which is to encourage U.S.-educated physicians to practice in underserved rural parts of the country, like Tioga and Crosby," Conrad said.

With a projected nationwide shortage of 200,000 physicians by 2020, small towns are already feeling the pinch of fewer candidates.

As Urvand said, "It's not a whole lot of names, and a lot of places are competing for them."

05/15/2006 09:17 FAX 7017461990 SENATOR CONRAD-GF → DC PRESS 002/006

Grand Forks

5/14/06

2D

KL

their **Opinion**

Do what it takes to get doctors

BISMARCK — The problem of securing physician services gives gray hairs and ulcers to administrators and board members of small, rural hospitals. The difficulty is nothing new, but it keeps getting more pronounced.

The situation was profiled recently in an article in the Crosby (N.D.) Record, specifically about the slimming numbers of physicians coming from Canada or other countries who are willing to serve Crosby's hospital.

A while back, there would be 150 applicants for an opening. Now, according to the article, quoting the administrator, there only have been a few indications of interest. The vacancy has lasted six months and continues.

It's not as if the shortage caught people unaware or that people haven't been working to find solutions, working industriously and creatively.

They've encountered a discouraging number of rocks and hard places.

It's proving harder to recruit a physician to live and practice in a small rural town when the spouse can't find a job in a specific professional field and the kids became used to big-city recreation and culture during the doctor's residency years. Also, a doctor may yearn to have a colleague nearby who, like her, is from India — but there's not another for long, lonely miles.

And the first doctor's spouse says, "Please don't make us go there."

Perhaps, as happens to some degree now, it will mean agreeing that the medical doctor and his family from another country will live in Minot or Bismarck-Mandan, and the doc will travel to rural clinics and hospitals. Transportation costs could be heavy, but technological advances in remote care medicine may help. Granted, it's being tried.

There have been good efforts made toward making it attractive for doctors from foreign places to find reason to serve rural patients. One of the most farsighted has been the State 30 Program, authored by Sen. Kent Conrad, D-N.D., in 1994 and renewed several times since, that gives each state 30 slots for foreign medical graduates to receive J1 waivers — visas — to live and practice in underserved areas for specified periods without necessarily having to enter the path to citizenship.

North Dakota has benefited. The country, particularly rural America, has benefited. In 2003, the Conrad State 30 program placed more than 1,000 physicians in underserved areas in the United States.

Designating qualifying small rural facilities as Critical Access Hospitals has helped. There are 31 in North Dakota in places such as Linton and Garrison, and yes, in Crosby. The status makes it much easier to get solid Medicare reimbursement money.

Wise heads in the health care community and government now need to come together to envision the next thing to try, the next program to get physicians to treat rural patients — whatever works.

— The Bismarck Tribune

2006 09:11 CONRAD BIS OFFICE 701 258 1254 P.05

Bismarck 6A (5-16-06)

Placing rural physicians a challenge

By ROBERT W. BEATTIE
Grand Forks

I read the May 9 editorial in the Bismarck Tribune with interest. There are many challenges to placing physicians in rural North Dakota. Actually, the overall challenge of physician recruitment is not isolated to just rural areas. Physician recruitment and retention is one of the primary challenges healthcare providers face, both in North Dakota and nationally.

The University of North Dakota School of Medicine and Health Sciences (UNDSMHS) recently celebrated its 100th year of preparing North Dakotans for a career in health care.

LETTERS TO THE EDITOR

Overall, the UNDSMHS has done a commendable job at providing physicians for North Dakota. Currently some 624 out of 1,417, or 45 percent, of practicing physicians in North Dakota have been trained by UNDSMHS. Nearly 60 percent of practicing family physicians in this state are graduates of our training programs. Using Bismarck as an example, 102 of the practicing physicians are graduates of UND.

There may not be an overall solution to the rural placement challenges for reasons cited by the editorial, perceived family needs, professional isolation and periodic breaks from the demands of practice.

The School of Medicine and Health Sciences offers a couple of avenues to address rural needs. One is the school itself, as a supplier of physicians and physicians assistants. Second is training that introduces third-year medical students to rural communities, through a program titled ROME (Rural Opportunities in Medical Education). ROME consists of a seven-month interdisciplinary experience in a rural primary care setting. Students live and train in the communities of Williston, Jamestown, Devils Lake and Hettinger, under the supervision of local physician preceptors.

Consistent with our tradition, the UNDSMHS will continue to be a leader in rural physician training.

(Beattie, a medical doctor, is a faculty member in the University of North Dakota School of Medicine and Health Sciences. — Editor)

PREPARED STATEMENT OF GREGORY SISKIND, CHAIRMAN, NATIONAL HEALTH CARE ACCESS COALITION

Statement of the National Health Care Access Coalition

On H.R. 4997,

The Physicians for Underserved Areas Act

Before the House Judiciary Committee
Subcommittee on Immigration, Border Security and Claims

May 18, 2006

Gregory Siskind
Chairman, National Health Care Access Coalition
901-682-6455
gsiskind@visalaw.com

The National Health Care Access Coalition is an organization comprised of health care employers, physicians and attorneys who advocate for physician immigration. We have worked for more than a decade to bring crucial physician immigration issues to the attention of Congress and we have worked with the various state and federal agencies that play a role in physician immigration to improve the process.

We support H.R. 4997 and believe it is crucial to ensuring access to health care for thousands of communities across America.

After the American students fill these positions, there are still 5,000 to 7,000 positions available in these graduate medical programs. These remaining slots are made available to graduates of foreign medical schools. And a substantial portion of this pool of international medical graduates (IMGs) comes to the US on the J-1 visa. A key requirement of J visa is that the doctor returns to his or her home country for two years upon completion of their program. A doctor agreeing to serve three years in a medically underserved community can remain in the US, however, with the support of an interested federal agency or, under the Conrad 30 J-1 waiver program, a state health agency.

On June 1, 2006, the Conrad 30 program is set to begin its sunset. Since the vast majority of J-1 waivers for doctors are granted by state health agencies, this will effectively end underserved area waivers for foreign physicians. Given the fact that thousands of communities around the US have benefited from J-1 waivers over the last two decades and given the well-recognized physician shortage in the US, this would represent a dramatic policy change for the country.

We believe that the J-1 Conrad waiver program has proven its worth and that instead of allowing the program to sunset, it should be permanently reauthorized and improved to allow even more doctors to remain in the US to provide valuable services to communities in need across America.

The Physician Shortage

Major organizations from the American Medical Association to the Council on Graduate Medical Education to the American Hospital Association to the Association of American Medical Colleges all agree that there is a serious physician shortage that will rise to crisis proportions over the next 15 years.

However, the shortage may be so severe that our best efforts may not be enough to solve the problem. According to the Health Policy Institute, the gap between available physicians and those needed by the country will expand to nearly 200,000. There are currently fewer than 800,000 physicians in the country so this shortage is large enough that it will likely affect most Americans.

The shortage can be blamed on numerous factors including

- The country's population is aging rapidly and the number of elderly Americans is growing much faster than the physician supply;

- The overall US population has grown by nearly 30 million since the last US medical school opened

- Technological advances have made numerous new medical treatments available that have increased the demand for physician services

- According to AAMC, the physician workforce is also aging. Today, approximately 200,000 doctors – nearly 1/3 of all active US physicians -- are over 55;

- Younger physicians are choosing to work shorter hours than their predecessors; and

- Half of the new medical doctors are women and they are gravitating to "controllable lifestyle" specialties (particularly primary care). They are also generally working fewer hours and seeing fewer patients per hour than their male counterparts and are frequently leaving the profession either temporarily or permanently when they have children. And studies show they are less likely to be attracted to rural positions thus making the shortages even worse in those communities.

This shortage will lead to a number of very serious problems for American patients:

- Long waits to see physicians;
- Skyrocketing physician salaries which, in turn, will put inflationary pressure on health care costs and availability of health insurance;
- Refusals by physicians to see Medicare and Medicaid patients;
- Lack of locally available physicians to an increasingly large geographic section of the country; and
- Increasing gap in availability of doctors between wealthy communities that can afford higher physician salaries and impoverished communities that cannot compete financially.

These issues are not unique to the United States. Much of the developing world has an aging population, women have had greater access to joining the health care profession, and many of the other factors mentioned earlier in this article apply outside the US as well as in the US. In fact, the US is not the leader when it comes to the percentage of our doctors who are international medical graduates.

According to the World Health Organization, the leader in recruiting IMGs is New Zealand with 34% of its doctors being educated elsewhere and the United Kingdom closely following at 33%. Australia's IMG population is 21% and Canada is at 23%. The US falls in the middle of this pack.

The reality is that while the US may feel guilty about recruiting physicians trained in developing countries and possibly exacerbating a brain drain in some markets, the fact is a doctor will often choose to go to another developing country if they are not permitted to remain in the US. Several countries, Australia being a prime example, have recently instituted "red carpet" visa programs to make it easy for physicians trained in the US to move there. The question then becomes not whether we should force doctors to leave so they can go home but whether we should be subsidizing the training of doctors for wealthy competitor countries.

The only true way to address a brain drain is to address the push factors that cause a doctor to immigrate – poor working conditions, civil unrest, crime, corruption, etc. Until living conditions and career opportunities improve in a country, a physician will rationally make the choice to emigrate. And if a physician is going to emigrate, the question then becomes how to make the US the destination to help address our own country's shortage.

The Role of J-1 Physicians in Addressing the Shortage

There are thousands of stories – some small, some great – of J-1 waiver doctors who have saved lives and dramatically improved the quality of life in communities across the country.

Examples include

- Osmond Hospital in Osmond, Nebraska. According to CEO Celine Mlady:

  "Without this program our hospital would be in dire straits. We recently recruited a foreign born physician and because of this program are working towards having him start work mid summer. We recruited for several months and had absolutely no interest from American born physicians. I am very grateful that this program exists."

- Cumberland Medical Center in Crossville, TN. According to Vice President Ronald Bodary:

  We have tried to recruit American born and trained specialty physicians, but were unsuccessful in our efforts or if we were able to recruit we could not retain them. In the past 2-5 years, through the Conrad Program we have successfully recruited an Endocrinologist, a Neurologist, a Rheumatologist and a Pulmonologist to our rural community. Each of these physicians have become a vital part of the community and hospital serving patients from our county as well as five other surrounding counties who do not offer these services. In addition, when we were more underserved and had access to primary care physicians, we were able to replace retiring physicians through that program. We have retained 7 physicians through that program who are active practitioners in this community providing access to care for patients in the Upper Cumberlands.

- Just this week, the *Denver Post* reported on Dr Saeid Ahmadpour, a physician in Cheyenne Wells, Colorado who is the only physician serving the county. The article quoted various members of the community who described the doctor's importance:

  "He's keeping us alive."
  "The doctor's fantastic."
  "Without a physician, our [nursing] home is in jeopardy."

How can physician immigration rules be changed to ameliorate the situation?

The National Healthcare Access Coalition makes the following recommendations for extension and improvement of the Conrad 30 waiver program.

1. Permanently Authorize the Conrad Program.

We suggest prompt passage of H.R. 4997 and applaud Congressman Moran and Pomeroy for their work on this important program. The Conrad 30 physician waiver provisions have now been operating for 12 years. Every state in the country has created a program, which has enabled states to bring physicians to the neediest areas of the U.S. Not a single state has terminated its participation in the program. This demonstrates that state health departments across the country view Conrad 30 as a valuable tool in addressing the severe physician shortage facing the country.

This program was initially created on a pilot basis to allow Congress to periodically evaluate its benefits. The active participation by all 50 states indicates this is no longer in question. Therefore, it is appropriate that the Conrad Program be permanently extended at this time.

2. Increase the Size of the Conrad Program to 40 Slots Per State

The Health Policy Institute, the leading think tank in the US studying the supply of physicians, projects a shortfall of 200,000 physicians by 2020. The Conrad 30 Program's maximum 1500 slots per year will come nowhere close to significantly alleviating this shortage. An expansion of slots (or even the elimination of a quota) is justified given the long term shortage prospects.

3. Allow Unused Slots to Be Used by States That Need Them

Unused Conrad 30 slots should be able to be "re-deposited" by willing states to be reclaimed by states that fill up their programs. In exchange for each re-deposited slot, a state giving up space in its program will be able to convert a remaining space to a flexibility slot, i.e., allowing the state to place the physician in the most needed location. This is an approach that was suggested by State 30 Administrators at their most recent annual meeting in Washington, DC.

4. Create An Extension of the Conrad Program for Academic Medical Centers

University medical centers play a vital role in nearly every state in the country. They often provide highly specialized health care services to large geographic areas and they engage in cutting edge research that is needed in a world facing pandemics and other health care crises. Some academic medical centers that by chance happen to be in physician shortage areas can qualify for Conrad 30 waivers. But many of these facilities have large numbers of physicians concentrated in a small college town and are unable to qualify as underserved. So they are left unable to recruit the brightest doctors who train in this country. Those doctors frequently are left with no choice but to go to competitor institutions abroad. And even when academic medical centers can qualify for waivers, they often are put in the untenable position of having to compete with rural areas for a precious Conrad slot. An expansion of the Conrad Program by ten slots reserved for America's research hospitals would greatly alleviate this problem.

5. Improve the Supply of Physicians to Katrina-Affected Areas

Many towns in the Gulf Coast region had difficulty finding enough doctors before Hurricane Katrina devastated the region. Katrina has turned this shortage into an immediate health care emergency. One of the less publicized effects of the storm has been the dramatic decline in the number of doctors in the area. Many physicians who evacuated quickly found jobs in other regions (not difficult given the overall national physician shortage) and physician groups that took years to build were dismantled overnight. Many hospitals in the Gulf Coast closed and displaced populations that may or may not return to their towns make returning to the Gulf Coast a risky proposition for doctors. Physician immigration can help alleviate the problem. Among the possible solutions are creating a blanket shortage area designation for the entire region, allowing affected communities unlimited numbers of Conrad waiver slots, extending the jurisdiction of the Delta Regional Authority and lowering the national interest waiver commitment time in Katrina areas to three years.

6. Streamline Processing of Waivers and Green Cards for Conrad Doctors

A. Remove physicians from the EB-2 Cap

In October 2005, the EB-2 permanent residency category began to "retrogress" for the first time in five years. Currently, physicians from India and China must wait at least five years for a green card to become available. That backlog in visa availability is expected to extend to doctors of all nationalities this spring and the waits could stretch several years longer based on current projections.

Part of the bargain of the Conrad Program is that, in exchange for serving three or more years, in an underserved area, a physician will be able to have a clear path to permanent residency. Without available green cards, the Conrad Program's attractiveness will be diminished greatly.

This backlog is already having the effect of causing many physicians to reconsider plans to work in underserved communities in the U.S. and instead pursue opportunities in other nations like the United Kingdom, Germany and Australia. To compete with these developed nations for the best doctors, we recommend removing physicians altogether from the EB-2 immigrant visa cap.

B. Authorize Physicians on H-1B Visas to Work in Underserved Areas

An increasing number of physicians are entering the U.S. on H-1B visas instead of J-1 visas. Many of these doctors would like to work in underserved communities upon conclusion of their training, but are not able to accept such positions because of the H-1B cap provisions. We recommend allowing an exemption from the H-1B cap for doctors who agree to work in underserved areas.

Given the well-documented severe shortage of doctors in the US that is expected to last at least twenty years, there is no rational reason to lump physicians in with workers in other occupations.

Conclusions:

It will be virtually impossible to avoid the effects of this "perfect storm." Instead, we would suggest that Congress pursue all avenues available to expand the supply of qualified doctors and not allow any of our existing sources of physicians to decline.

There is no one who can credibly say that international medical graduates can alone solve the physician shortage, nor would most physician immigration advocates criticize embarking on a strategy to address the shortage that included graduating more American medical doctors and doctors of osteopathy and increasing the availability of non-physicians to assume duties that can be realistically and safely be undertaken without a medical degree.

The US should be actively promoting both increasing the number of medical schools and medical school slots. And we need to be creating more opportunities for IMGs to remain in the US when their training is finished and not making a bad situation worse by cutting off a reliable source of physicians on which the US depends. It would be a tragic mistake to take steps today that would actually decrease the availability of IMGs including not extending the Conrad 30 waiver program.

We support prompt passage of H.R. 4997.

Attachment: List of Supporters

List of Supporters of the Conrad State 30 Program[1]

1. Associations and Organizations:

The American Hospital Association
The American Thoracic Society
The Association of Staff Physician Recruiters
The Delta Regional Authority
The National Health Care Access Coalition

2. Hospitals and Health Care Providers:

Arizona: The Mayo Clinic
Scottsdale/Phoenix

California: Clinicas Del Ramno Real
Ventura, CA

Clinicas de Salud Del Pueblo
Brawley, CA

Golden Valley Health Centers
Merced, CA

Shasta County Dept. of Health
Shasta, CA

Mountain Valley Health Centers
Bieber, CA

Connecticut: Danbury Office of Physician Services
Danbury, CN

Florida: Florida Hospital Heartland Medical Center
Sebring, FL

Rose Fernandez
Community Health Centers
Dade City and Lakeland,

The Mayo Clinic
Jacksonville, FLA

[1] As of May 16, 2006, as indicated by letters to Congress or email confirmation to the National Health Care Access Coalition.

Illinois:	Crusader Clinic Rockford, IL
	Methodist Medical Center of IL Peoria, IL
	Aunt Martha Youth Service Center Chicago, IL
	Heartland Community Health Center Peoria, IL
	Central Counties Health Center Springfield, IL
Indiana:	St. Margaret Mercy Healthcare Centers Dyer and Hammond, IN
	Terre Haute Pulmonary Terre Haute, IN
Iowa:	Cedar Valley Medical Specialists, P.C. Waterloo, IA
Kansas:	Coffeyville Regional Medical Center Coffeyville, KS
	Kiowa County Memorial Hospital Greenburg, KS
	Preferred Medical Associates Wichita, KS
Kentucky:	University of Louisville Louisville, KY
	Appalachian Clinic(s) Hazard and Wooton, KY
	Appalachian Regional Heathcare Lexington and Hazard, KY

	Kentucky River Medical Center Jackson, KY
	Marymount Medical Center London, KY
Louisiana:	Rapides Regional Medical Center Alexandria, LA
Massachusetts:	Baystate Medical Center Springfield, MA
	Franklin Medical Center Greenfield, MA
	Holyoke Hospital Holyoke, MA
Minnesota:	The Mayo Clinic Rochester, MN
	Dr. Surjit Moolamalla Arlington, MN
Mississippi:	Family Health Center Sandersville, MS
	Madison County Medical Center Canton, MS
	Access Family Health Center Smithville, MS
	Southwest MS Regional Medical Center McComb, MS
	Family Health Center Laurel, MS
	Trace Regional Hospital Houston, MS

Delta Regional Medical Center
Greenville, MS

North Mississippi Health Services
Tupelo, MS

Greater Meridian Health Clinic, Inc.
Meridian, Shuqualuk, DeKalb, Louisville, Scooba, and Starkville, MS

Pine Belt Mental Health Care Resources
Hattiesburg, MS

Warren-Yazoo Mental Health Service
Vicksburg, MS

Grenada Lake Medical Center
Grenada, MS

Weems Community Mental Health Center
Meridian, MS

Northwest Mississippi Regional Medical Center
Clarksdale, MS

HeartSouth
Hattiesburg, MS

Calhoun Health Services
Calhoun City, MS

All Children's Clinic
Senatobia, MS

Nebraska: Faith Regional Health Services
Norfolk, NE

Nebraska Hospital Association

Osmond General Hospital
Osmond, NE

BryanLGH Enterprises, aka Bryant LGH Health System
Lincoln, NE

New York: Columbia University/NY Presbyterian Hospital
New York, New York

	Mount Sinai Medical Center New York, New York
	Woodhull Medical & Mental Health Center Brooklyn, New York
N. Carolina:	Tri-County Community Health Council Dunn, NC
Ohio:	Cleveland Clinic Foundation Cleveland, OH
Oklahoma:	Univ. of Oklahoma Health Science Center Department of Surgery Oklahoma City, OK
Pennsylvania:	Univ. of Pittsburgh Medical Center Pittsburgh, PA
	Univ. of Pennsylvania Health System Cardiovascular Division Philadelphia, PA
	Keystone Health Center Chambersburg, PA
	Haverford Anesthesia Associates, PC Havertown, PA
	Hahnemann University Hospital (Tenet) Philadelphia, PA
S. Carolina:	Hampton Regional Medical Hampton, SC
South Dakota:	Sioux Valley Clinic Sioux Falls, SD
Tennessee:	St. Jude Children's Research Hospital Memphis, TN
	Cumberland Medical Center Crossville, TN

University of Tennessee Health Science Center
Memphis, TN

Community Health Systems
Brentwood, TN [74 hospitals in 22 states]

Texas:

Premier Family Care
Midland, TX

Midland Memorial Hospital
Midland, TX

Univ. of Texas Medical Branch at Galveston
Galveston, TX

Pecos County Memorial Hospital
Fort Stockton, TX

Family Medical Center
Kermit, TX

Winkler County Memorial Hospital
Kermit, TX

Kellum Medical Group
San Antonio, Lytle, Lake Hills, TX

Virginia:

Lee Regional Medical Center
Pennington Gap, VA

Halifax Regional Hospital
South Boston, VA

Wisconsin:

Aurora Medical Group/Aurora Health Care, Inc.
Milwaukee, WI
Largest Private Employer in Wisconsin
Hospitals and Clinics throughout eastern Wisconsin

Bay Area Medical Center
Marinette, WI

Milwaukee Health Services, Inc.
Milwaukee, WI

16th Street Community Health Center
Milwaukee, WI

LETTER TO THE HONORABLE SHEILA JACKSON LEE FROM CONNIE BERRY, MANAGER, TEXAS PRIMARY CARE OFFICE

TEXAS DEPARTMENT OF STATE HEALTH SERVICES

EDUARDO J. SANCHEZ, M.D., M.P.H.
COMMISSIONER

1100 W. 49th Street • Austin, Texas 78756
1-888-963-7111 • http://www.dshs.state.tx.us

May 12, 2006

The Honorable Sheila Jackson Lee
United States House of Representatives
2435 Rayburn House Office Building
Washington, D.C. 20515-4318

Dear Representative Jackson Lee:

In response to a request from Nolan Rappaport of your staff, I am providing information explaining the need for additional J-1 waiver slots in Texas. This is provided for your information in advance of the upcoming House Subcommittee on Immigration and Border Security Hearing on the Conrad State 30 program.

A Health Professional Shortage Area (HPSA) is a designation made by the Secretary of the Department of Health and Human Services (DHHS) and indicates that the area has a ratio of one primary care physician or less per 3,500 people, or per 3,000 people if there is high poverty in the area. There are also low-income and facility HPSAs using federal criteria, as well as Medically Underserved Areas and Populations. These designations also have a federally defined criteria.

According to DHHS, Texas has the second highest number of HPSAs in the country, with 346 designated in the state. This is one less HPSA than California, which has 10 million more people than Texas. Additionally, the National Health Service Corps (a DHHS program for recruiting health professionals) indicates that 1,316 primary care physicians are needed in Texas to achieve a ratio of 2,000 people per physician. The designation only measures access to primary health care and not specialists. According to Dr. Kenneth Shine, Executive Vice Chancellor for Health Affairs at the University of Texas System, looking at all physician specialties, in 2004 there were approximately 228 physicians per 100,000 population for the United States, while in Texas, the ratio was 155 physicians per 100,000, or 30% below the national average.

Texas is trying to do its part by training physicians for our state and the rest of the country. Currently, there are 2,555 doctors in primary care residency programs in Texas. The number of International Medical Graduates is 798 or 31% of primary care residents. The limitation on the number of Conrad 30 waivers per state allows Texas to request waivers for only 30 of the foreign residents who complete training each year, and yet each year the state could place an additional 50 Conrad 30 doctors in Texas where they are trained and greatly needed.

In previous years, Texas relied heavily on the United States Department of Agriculture (USDA) J-1 waiver program. Through this program, USDA processed 424 applications for waivers in Texas, with 297 recommendations between 1994 and 2000. After completing their three-year obligation, 84.5% of the 297 doctors remained in Texas and 80% of the 297 doctors remained working in the HPSA where they were recommended. After the USDA program ended in March 2002, and before Texas decided to participate in the Conrad 30 program, our office looked at this data and determined that the visa waiver program was a useful tool to address physician shortages in underserved areas. The small number of Conrad program slots, which was 20 at the time Texas started recommending waivers, has always been a concern because it limits the state to improving access in such a small number of our underserved and shortage areas.

Most of our Texas Conrad 30 doctors are still within the three-year obligation. Of the 131 Conrad 30 waivers recommended since April 2002, only one was non-compliant, three returned to their home countries and two were granted Conrad 30 waivers in other states. We have had program compliance and satisfaction with 95% of the doctors and their sponsors.

In addition to recruiting and retaining health professionals in Texas, the Texas Primary Care Office has worked to capture the national "snap shot" of the Conrad 30 program. We survey states annually to determine the number of waiver recommendations made by each state, as well as individual state policies and procedures, and prepare summaries of the survey results. Additionally, the office convenes Conrad 30 programs in conjunction with other national meetings. These meetings include representatives from Department of Homeland Security, Department of State, other waiver programs such as the Appalachian Regional Commission and DHHS. A Conrad 30 Group website is facilitated by our office to provide an opportunity for the Conrad 30 programs to share information, ask questions, and learn from other states. This site is also a tool for other agencies and commissions to seek data and information about the program and its impact nationally.

Thank you for this opportunity to talk about the importance of the Conrad/State 30 program to Texas. We can expand and improve access to health care for our communities if allowed the opportunity to recommend additional J-1 visa waivers. If you have any additional questions, please contact me at (512) 458-7518 or connie.berry@dshs.state.tx.us.

Sincerely,

Connie Berry, Manager
Texas Primary Care Office

cc: Eduardo Sanchez, Texas Department of State Health Services
Stephanie Muth, Texas Health and Human Services Commission